THE BILLBOARD GUIDE TO

MUSIC
Publicity

REVISED EDITION

THE BILLBOARD GUIDE TO

MUSIC Publicity

REVISED EDITION

JIM PETTIGREW, JR.

BILLBOARD BOOKS
An imprint of Watson-Guptill Publications/New York

Senior Editor: Bob Nirkind
Edited by: Amy Handy
Book and cover design: Bob Fillie, Graphiti Graphics
Production Manager: Hector Campbell

Copyright © 1997 by Jim Pettigrew, Jr.

First published 1997 by Billboard Books, an imprint of Watson-Guptill Publications,
a division of BPI Communications, Inc., 770 Broadway, New York, NY 10003

All rights reserved. No part of this publication may be reproduced, stored in a retrieval system,
or transmitted, in any form or by any means—electronic, mechanical, photocopying, recording,
or otherwise—without prior permission of the publisher.

Library of Congress Cataloging-in-Publication Data
Pettigrew, Jim
     The Billboard guide to music publicity/ Jim Pettigrew, Jr.—Rev. ed.
        p.   cm.
     Rev. ed. of: The Billboard guide to music publicity
     Includes index.
     ISBN 0-8230-7626-1
     1. Music publicity. I. Pettigrew, Jim. Billboard guide to music publicity.
  II. Title
  ML3790.P47 1997
  659.2'978—dc21   96-49873
                                   CIP
                                   MN

Manufactured in the United States of America

First printing, 1997

3 4 5 6 7 8 9 / 05 04 03 02 01 00

To the loving memory of my mother, Ellen,
and my brother, Larry.
They loved all kinds of music.

ACKNOWLEDGMENTS

First, I'd like to thank my former editor, Paul Lukas, for his input and assistance during the planning stages of this revision. I also want to thank Bob Nirkind, my current editor, for his remarkable insight, care, and patience. I am deeply grateful to my wife, Mary Ellen, and my daughter, Danellen, for their patience and support during the evolution of this book.

Special credit is also due to three people with whom I worked closely in music PR, coming to know them as dedicated professionals: Howard Bloom, Mike Hyland, and Mark Pucci. My profound gratitude also goes to my parents, Jim and Ellen, for their musical heritage and unceasing support. Through her last days, my mother was a beacon of strength for this project, my number one fan.

Three special people were very generous with their support during the span of this project: Dr. Linda Coleman, Mary Dan, and Bob Miller. A unique gratitude is due to my friend Marshall Allen, who transcribed the interviews.

Several friends deserve more than my appreciation. They went out of their way during this project, to keep my machines running and upgraded, to offer assistance and sounding boards, and, in each case, true literate comradeship. They are Charlie Raiford, Russell Shaw, James T. Bass, Stanley Booth, Bill Diehl, Russ Holloway, Frank Sawyer, Dr. Ted Blau, Michael Henderson, Susan Harte, and Mark Mayfield.

Many thanks to my friend Stanley Booth, for his kind words to open this book.

My sincere appreciation also goes to the members of the Golden Isles Writers' Group and to the members of the Golden Isles Lions Club, for their camaraderie and support.

I am grateful to all the people whose thoughts appear inside these pages. To a person, they graciously took time out from demanding schedules. Without their professional outlook, experience, and sense of ethics, the scope of this book would have been virtually impossible.

JIM PETTIGREW, JR.
St. Simons Island, Georgia
April 1996

CONTENTS

FOREWORD

One sad fact many artists learn is that it isn't enough just to master one's art—survival as an artist requires many skills, more than most people possess. No matter how well you sing, write, or play an instrument, chances are the world won't beat a path to your door. That is, unless someone is in the lead, saying, "It's this way! Follow me! You gotta hear this!" How do you get someone to do that? Read this book and find out.

Jim Pettigrew has done publicity work for some of the biggest names in the music business, among them the Allman Brothers Band and ZZ Top, and he knows what he's talking about. This guide is a practical, useful tool with hundreds of wise suggestions, designed to get artists where they want to go and to keep them there. It answers more questions than any musician is likely to have about all relevant subjects, from how to get 8 x 10 glossies to what to say on the *Today* show. If you're a musician or any sort of entertainment business professional, you need to know what's in this book. It's costing you money not to know. In clear, concise, easily understood prose, with good sense and good humor, Jim Pettigrew gives you the weapons to survive in the jungle of modern music.

Reading the book won't make you rich and famous, but if you read it and do what it says, you'll be way ahead of anyone who hasn't.

STANLEY BOOTH, JR.
author, *The True Adventures of the Rolling Stones,*
Rythm Oil, and *Keith: Standing in the Shadows*

INTRODUCTION

It's a familiar situation in the world of pop music: you find yourself working as a manager with a rock band or a shy poet-singer. The act records well, plays well onstage, and has begun to gather a following. But it soon becomes apparent that similar acts with other companies are getting a lot more press coverage than yours.

So what do you do? Ignore the situation and concentrate on getting the equipment truck back from the repo man? Or do you treat the problem as serious enough to warrant your immediate attention and decide that better publicity may be the key to your artist's ability to compete?

This basic scenario may be played out in several different ways within the business of recorded music. You may be starting in an entry-level position in a music PR office. Your first visit reveals a highly charged atmosphere of glamour, rapid-fire phone conversations, and a high level of tension. How do you approach the situation so that you make a good impression and don't come off as hopelessly inexperienced?

Or you may be an experienced publicist. Before the first cup of coffee has gone cold, you learn that you are now the proud account rep of a problem act, with problems on the road, at home, and at the label. What are your options? Do you quit and go back to school? Or do you walk to the gym and start thinking about how to meet this challenging task head on?

Or you may be a member of a band who has achieved some degree of success on a local level and is ready to start eliciting attention from some major labels. What are the first steps you should take? Back to the garage to work on your forty-first demo tape? Or to a professional PR agent to start putting together an effective press kit and production materials?

THE VALUE OF PUBLICITY

Over the years a debate has existed in the music industry about the importance of publicity. Some managers play it down, flatly refusing all press requests for interviews, thinking that such procedures are needless bothers. Other managers have welcomed press interest, eager to get the added exposure.

Today, the powerful role of publicity in the pop music world is incontestable. The competitive nature of the music business is more intense now than ever before, and the artist with the best-planned overall career strategy and a professional approach to getting noticed stands a better chance of achieving success.

Nowadays the psychology of fans and the basic psychology of sales are better understood by music executives. If music fans hear a CD on the radio, chances are they won't recognize the artist—or buy the CD—if that's the only exposure they've had to the act. But if fans have recently seen a story on the group in their favorite music or pop-culture magazine, the odds of their buying the CD are much greater.

The same simple psychological concept is true for other purchasing decisions. How can a rock band or solo artist be interested in a particular recording studio if they've never heard of it, or never seen a story in a music trade magazine about it?

So publicity is a vital component of any effective success strategy in the music business. Knowledge of professional PR is important throughout the industry— not just for publicity people. *Everyone* who is currently working in the music industry, or who wishes to enter the field, should have a basic awareness of what publicity is and how it works. It is crucial, for example, that musicians know how to act when talking to reporters or facing TV cameras. And managers must now be aware of all the options that properly executed PR can add to an artist's career. The same goes for record-company executives and concert promoters, who should know what publicity can and cannot do for their label or company. And the axiom applies to people on the technical side. If you're in lighting or sound, or if you are a producer or engineer, you should be cognizant of how media exposure can enhance your business or boost your career.

Regardless of your position or career goals, and even if you will never make, or answer, a publicity call, you should know something about the reality of public relations and the media. With a clear understanding of PR basics, you will know when it's being done correctly for you and your clients. And if you are considering a career in the music business, it'll be worth your while to take a look at the publicity end; it offers plenty of excitement, constant challenge, and lots of room for creativity.

To that end, this book is offered, and it aims to fully examine contemporary public relations in the entertainment world.

PART 1

THE HUNT FOR EXPOSURE

1

A PUBLICITY OVERVIEW

To some people, the product of publicity in the music business can be described in a single word: hype.

The term is a common one in the entertainment industry. It refers to the attention-grabbing strategies and abnormally inflated language used to increase an artist's exposure in the media. Over the years hype has taken many forms under the publicity seeker's pen: the use of overblown adjectives to describe an artist's work; exaggerated accounts of how a rock band got together; the spicing up of a musician's career story in order to make it more interesting. All of these techniques, and more, have been applied to the problem of how to promote an artist's career in the wildly competitive field of music and entertainment.

But publicity in today's world involves much more than hype. In terms of required strategies, the search for attention in the music business could be compared to a sophisticated board game, full of tricks and pitfalls for the unwary, but also holding lots of rewards for the sharp-witted (and those in a position to capitalize on luck).

Despite its gamelike similarities, however, music PR and publicity is now a very serious business, with very real stakes and its own set of professional requirements. The techniques and tools of gaining attention in the media have finally taken some fairly concrete shapes and can be presented in terms of recommended procedures and guidelines.

THE BUSINESS OF ATTRACTING ATTENTION

You may see the activity referred to as public relations, publicity, public information, press relations, or PR, but all the terms mean the same thing. Regardless of the phrase, this field involves the professional management of a client's media exposure, or, put more plainly, the process of working with the mass media to bring an act to the public's attention.

This exposure can come in many different forms. It may be a cover story in a major music magazine, a record review in the music section of a big-city newspaper, an interview on a nationally syndicated radio show, an appearance on a local TV noonday show, a one-line mention in an entertainment column, or numerous other examples, such as a forty-five-second slot on "Entertainment Tonight" or an in-depth profile in a technical publication. The job of the publicity seeker is often to aim for *all* of the above.

THE IMPORTANCE OF PUBLICITY

No one can argue the critical importance of radio and TV airplay and live performances to the career of the professional musician. Without this basic communication, the artist is working in a vacuum. But with regard to the nonmusical form of publicity, some managers, musicians, and record companies have curiously regarded it as a kind of lost cousin of the industry—a troublesome afterthought at best. In some cases this attitude stemmed from fear and mistrust, in other cases from simple ignorance of the ways this added exposure to the public can help a particular client.

Among most music business professionals today, however, the attitude toward publicity is quite different. Music-business professionals recognize that a well-conceived and well-executed PR plan is a valuable and integral part of an artist's career schematic (or of a nonartist client's business strategy).

Publicity and recognition are vital for a number of reasons, not least of which is the state of competition in the contemporary music industry. It exists in every aspect of the business: the competition is stiff for radio airtime, TV slots, and the public's purchase dollar for concert tickets and recorded music.

A well-rounded PR approach can be a tremendous help in cutting a path through the competition. Exposure in the print and electronic media, for example, can favorably position the music group or other client and thus enhance CD and ticket sales. Similar publicity can also boost the volume of business at a recording studio or provide information that may incline an artist to sign with a particular label.

Recognition is a key element here. Fans who have only been exposed to the music of a new rock band, for example, are normally not that eager to go out and buy the album or CD. But if those same fans have also read about the act in their local newspaper or their favorite music magazine, they are often much more prone to make that all-important purchase decision.

Building up a "psychological imprint" of recognition and familiarity is extremely important for developing bands and other young or new musical entities. It's also important to the longevity of an established artist's career. Similarly, the public perception enhanced by media exposure can help define a "hot" record label or an "in" studio—separating them from the also-rans.

The viewpoint and insight provided by feature articles in newspapers, magazines, and TV talk show appearances are important in other ways. Information about a group's musical, social, spiritual, and political outlook can be of immense interest to a fan and again can lead to a buying decision. Followers of particular groups are also naturally interested in the band's lifestyle, for example, as well as the members' romances, road antics, protests, angers, frustrations, and musical motivations. Fans want to identify with pop-music groups when possible, and publicity exposure is the best way to accomplish this.

For established groups, professional PR serves a slightly different purpose. Fans tend already to know quite a lot about platinum and superstar acts, but they want to know more—and on a consistent basis. Here publicity can be an invaluable tool, answering such questions as: What's the new album about? How have the members' attitudes changed? What kind of expensive sports cars have they bought? What impossibly expensive and exotic vacation spots have they been to? Publicity exposure keeps open a line of communication between the act and its audience and can help to insure a longer, more successful career.

Publicity at this level can serve another purpose. It is often used to control the dissemination of information in a way that is favorable to a group's image. If various members of a band express differing opinions about a personnel change, for example, creating the public impression of confusion and disarray, a publicist can serve as a centralized source of information, providing only the opinions and facts that are helpful to the artist's career. (See Lesley Pitts's comments on page 151.)

Media exposure can also be valuable for nonperforming and corporate clients. Dance bands, religious pop groups, jazz singers, and other artists can't be expected to have interest in a particular producer unless they've read about him or her or heard about the person in some way. So publicity in trade journals and technical publications offers a vehicle through which people on the production and engineering side can reach their market.

The same reasoning applies to inanimate clients, such as recording studios and record labels. An important factor here is the volume of business and industry positioning. The competition between studios is particularly intense today. So the studio that has had its comfortable atmosphere and state-of-the art equipment featured in the technical press is most likely to come out on top in terms of business volume. Often emerging acts may want to record in a specific studio because a hot album was recently cut there, and publicity is the best way to get the word out, to exploit that studio's success.

A label's executives may decide to get involved in a big charity cause, purely for goodwill purposes. The results, properly exposed in the media, can manifest themselves in subtle ways. The music fan who has a good feeling about the label behind an act may be more psychologically inclined to buy their product.

WHAT THE PUBLICIST DOES

Public relations in contemporary entertainment has followed a trend toward specialization. In the music industry, promotion people seek radio airplay of CDs and other recorded material. Video specialists work directly with the numerous television shows that feature videos. Music publicists work in the rest of the mass media—a huge and complex arena of its own. Yet we use the term *entertainment* here because the lines of separation between pop music, film, stage, and TV are becoming increasingly vague, and publicity hounds may find themselves working in all four industries in the same day. The do-it-yourself promoter, of course, must be a jack-of-all-publicity-trades, familiarizing himself or herself with all the possible outlets for information about a band, and designing and preparing a wide array of print and electronic materials.

In an overall sense, entertainment public relations people are in the business of image. In the search to frame that image in the collective mind of the public, publicists immerse themselves in a process that has several phases. First, a publicist does extensive research to find out what profile the client has (even if the client is unaware of it or doesn't know how to handle it). Second, the PR professional devotes serious thought to how that image can be sharpened, clarified, and/or amplified. Next, he or she draws up a specific plan on how the client can be packaged, illuminated, and made attractive to the mass media. Finally, after this research and development phase, the PR person goes into the day-to-day work of managing the client's image, developing publicity materials and using communication tools. The goal of all this planning and work is to transform the client into an entity that is accessible and interesting, resulting in added coverage through various components of the mass media.

When things are done correctly, the results can be eye-popping in a national campaign—stories, reviews, headlines, and radio/TV exposure from coast to coast. And the publicist is rewarded with an immense amount of professional satisfaction in knowing that he or she set up lots of this coverage behind-the-scenes.

The best way to illustrate a publicity person's role is by placing it in the center of a diagram. Most often, the music publicist is in the middle of a constantly changing business relationship. He or she acts as a conduit between two entities. The client—a rock band, solo artist, record label, or studio—is on one side, with needs and demands. The media—magazines, TV, newspapers, and radio—is on the other side, with its own set of rules, needs and demands.

The successful publicity hunter must be keenly aware of both parties and their often-differing goals and viewpoints. On a day-to-day basis, the publicist attempts to match these needs and demands whenever possible. At times the

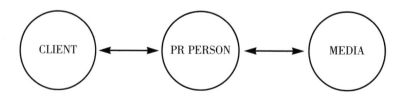

client may want exposure in a particular type of media and that media may or may not want to provide it. At other times the media may be hungry for particular subject matter and the publicist is then in the position of providing ready-made information. Whatever the situation, the role of the publicist is constantly evolving and rarely dull.

If the job of getting exposure in the media sounds impossible, it is certainly not. People willing to apply themselves and who are not afraid of hard work can enter the fray and have success. And those who aim for careers as music publicists will find an area of work that is cosmopolitan, interesting, and often rewarding—involving travel, meeting interesting people, and working in an environment that's almost never dull.

Any field in the music business is difficult to break into, but none of them are impossible. The true test is to establish a track record and carve out a long-term career. Continuing success and increasing recognition in the field are dependent upon reliability, tenacity, and an array of other personal qualities. In general, the person who develops the best reputation will get inside and stay inside the music business fast track.

The image of the music publicist as flaky party animal is coming to an end, as professionalism, business acumen, and more scientific approaches come to characterize the field. It's an exciting time to enter this field, and opportunites to participate abound.

2

A LOOK AT
THE MEDIA

Y ou don't have to be involved in the
publicity game very long to realize just how vast, powerful, and complex the
mass-media arena is today. The following data are drawn from *Gale's Directory of
Publications & Broadcast Media.*

- By the mid-1990s, in the United States alone, there were 1,520 TV stations,
  9,767 commercial radio stations, 1,791 noncommercial radio stations (mostly
  college), and 11,660 cable TV operators. On the World Wide Web, the graphical side of the Internet, there were 11,691 music-related sites by the mid-'90s,
  and growing very rapidly. (For more information, see the Shaw and Gillen
  interviews, pages 142 and 159.)

- On the print side, there were 1,537 daily newspapers, 7,655 weeklies (including freebies, ethnic, and alternatives), 662 college newspapers, plus some
  11,937 magazines and specialty publications. Together, these outlets reach an
  audience in the hundreds of millions.

Obviously, all these information entities are not accessible to the music publicity seeker at any one time, but the mass media represents a dizzying array of possibilities for attracting the attention of a huge body of people. And that is why so
many publicity people scramble so hungrily for airtime and editorial space.

THE ROLE OF THE MEDIA

The various components of the media, whether urban daily newspapers, national TV networks, or modest specialty magazines, are all in the business of communicating to an audience. Widely differing techniques are used, from the trashy
to the sublime, but the goal is still the same.

The twofold challenge that constantly faces publishers, editors, and journalists is to inform and entertain their audience. On the information or "hard news"
side, members of the media have a vitally important responsibility—to keep

readers, listeners, and viewers informed about serious current issues. This involves the seldom-easy task of reporting objectively and fairly on events, debates, and controversies that have gray areas of subtle complexity and are often not easily understood.

On the entertainment side, editors, writers, producers, and electronic hosts expend a great deal of effort to attract, hold, and engage an audience, and these efforts extend to music, movies, theater, TV, fiction, and humor. While it is perhaps not as crucial to society as hard news, the entertainment aspect of the media is quite important, and the competition is usually stiff for the audience's leisure or entertainment time. The field of music publicity most often involves working with contacts connected with the entertainment side—rather than the hard news side—of the media.

THE MEDIA/PUBLICIST RELATIONSHIP

In many ways the relationship between the media and the publicist is one of mutual dependence. We already know about the importance of magazines, newspapers, TV, and radio to the PR person. At the same time, the publicist fulfills an important need for the media.

Print and electronic editors face the constant challenge, on a daily basis, of filling pages and electronic time slots with interesting, controversial, shocking, and/or amusing material. The situation is much like a paper or electronic monster that's always hungry and can never be fully satiated. (An old joke in the newspaper industry goes, "Whew! Only 364 more issues to go.")

Simply put, if newspaper columnists, magazine editors, or talk-show producers feel that an item or subject is correct for their audience, it's quite likely that they will set aside some of their alloted space for it. Or the media person may file that item in a folder marked something like "Consider in the Immediate Future." Many times these decisions are made in a few seconds.

Conversely, if a TV entertainment reporter or music magazine editor feels that a new vocal-pop group or some other subject is too far out of their audience's taste, then they won't devote any of their space to it. A "no" decision can be made for numerous other reasons, such as a recent story run on a similar act, or because the editor feels the act is boring or has little to say artistically. Media professionals are constantly making decisions like this, keeping their audience as clearly defined as possible and offering material that the audience will pay attention to and be entertained by—whether they are intrigued, amused, or in some cases even shocked.

Regardless of their style or position, all media people need a constant flow of information, and quite often this is where publicists come in. Few people in the general public realize just how much American media content is generated by "PR plants" or information supplied by publicists. The magazine cover story on a rock group is usually tied in with a tour or an album release and is directly related to the efforts of the publicity office. An appearance by a celebrity on a talk show is often set up by a publicist to help promote a new film or book. PR reps frequently call magazine editors to offer interview opportunites with artists from their roster. Thus a contemporary journalism phrase, often heard around newsrooms and TV studios, begins to come into focus: "A PR hack is a pain in the ass, but a good PR person is invaluable."

The course of a professional relationship between a publicist and a media person can flow in several different directions. Ideally, the relationship remains friendly, straightforward, and mutually beneficial. The editor, having come to know and trust the publicist, may call often, seeking help on stories or looking for actual leads.

Or the relationship may be fraught with problems. Some of these can easily be rectified and others may border on the incurable. Certain editors (or producers, or reporters) may have a cynical attitude toward publicity people in general, regarding them as pests and saying no with trigger-happy frequency. Other media people, who know that the PR person is on the spot, may delight in being rude and abusive, knowing that the publicist usually cannot retaliate (not immediately, anyway). Some over-eager PR people may indeed tend to be pushy and turn into editorial headaches, while others, defensive about lackluster clients, may try to beg, whine, or threaten.

The list of possible relationships between media and PR people goes on and on, but this central fact remains: in one corner of the arena stands the media person, constantly charged with informing and entertaining an audience; in another corner is the publicist, who wants something from the editor for a selfish reason—namely, exposure for a client.

However delicate the situation may be, the media/publicist interaction is far from being unworkable. People crave entertainment, whether they admit it or not, and media people know this. The music publicist helps to feed the hungry beast.

Within this relationship, the professional publicist who retains a sense of ethics and who is versed in the proper techniques—and armed with all the current tools—can achieve a great deal of success, generating an enormous amount of exposure for a client.

ADVERTISING VERSUS EDITORIAL/PROGRAMMING

The media in the United States is currently made up of two sectors: commercial and noncommercial. Commercial outlets, by far the greater portion of the media, are supported by the sale of advertising space or time. Almost all of the print media, other than a few privately published newsletters and corporate publications, derive income from advertising space and newsstand sales or subscriptions.

On the electronic side, commercial TV and radio get their income solely from the sale of advertising time. Noncommercial radio and TV (National Public Radio and the Public Broadcasting System) are nonprofit and supported by viewer/listener donations, grants, and federal funds.

Apart from musical airplay and live concert footage, there are two basic types of exposure that may be gained through the media. The first, advertising, is page space or air time that's paid for by the client. The second, editorial space or programming time on-air, is free—and that is one of the reasons it is so strenuously sought after by publicists of all kinds, from corporate to music to charities.

Normally, newspaper/magazine publishers and electronic media general managers keep a strict delineation between what is advertising and what is editorial/programming. This is extremely important because advertisers are free (within certain limits) to say or imply whatever they wish in an advertisement. On the editorial/programming side, reporters, writers, and air personalities must be unhampered by advertiser pressure and able to criticize when editors deem it proper for the public good. This is a key factor in contemporary media ethics and a foundation point in the media's role as public watchdog.

Each type of exposure, advertising and editorial/programming, has its own definite uses and advantages. The music press agent must have a clear understanding of each, to help in the decision-making process.

Advertising

In pop music, as a general rule, advertising is used to "get the word out" in the sense of an announcement. Ad "insertions" or "time-buys" are normally utilized in a very timely way—to announce a single event of one kind or another. The type of musical event may vary widely: the release of a new CD; the debut of a new band; the opening of a recording studio; a concert tour kickoff date; the merger of two record companies; or the acquisition of a major artist by a new record company.

Music-business advertising may at times take particular stands, such as supporting an organization like Rock The Vote (RTV), or voicing industry opinions on issues that affect the music business, like anti-piracy or royalty legislation.

Advertising is very expensive and normally serves best in an announcement role. In most large music-business companies publicists have little or nothing to do with advertising, since it's handled by a different department. At small labels or "one-person-does-it-all" situations like the management of many new bands, the person handling publicity may also be taking care of a small amount of advertising. This is the exception, though, and not the rule.

Huge corporations may mount massive, long-running ad campaigns to influence public opinion, as they do with the introduction of a new automobile model. But in the music business, as a general rule, advertising does not perform well in an opinion-formation role. At the college level, for example, studies have shown that the credibility (believability) of advertising is rather low in pop music. Roughly 30 percent of fans who see or hear an ad about a new CD, for example, will actually believe that it's wonderful. Music advertising, though, can be very effective in stepping up sales momentum, as in the case of a new CD and tour already doing well.

Editorial

Programming time and editorial space, on the other hand, have a comparatively high credibility ratio—about 70 percent. Readers, listeners, and viewers are much more apt to think that a new CD is worth investigating, for example, if they're exposed to it on the editorial side. If a radio talk-show host mentions the new CD during an interview with the artist, or if the new release is treated favorably within a newspaper or magazine feature story, then the music fan is much more likely to consider making a purchase. The same concept applies to dozens of other exposure situations, including concert previews, album reviews, technical summaries in trade publications, and mentions in entertainment columns, to name just a few.

As with radio airplay and music-video time slots, it is difficult to overemphasize the enormous impact that added media exposure can have on an artist, or any other client.

SUMMARY

At this point, the challenge facing the publicity seeker should be in sharp focus. Like a giant carrot, the powerful exposure weapon of the mass media is dangling in front of the hungry PR person. But nothing in contemporary life is that simple—the media carrot is elusive and can't easily be touched. Eager publicists can't simply reach out and help themselves to all that delicious exposure. The profits of exposure are gained only through knowledge of the tools and skill in their preparation.

3

YOU, THE
PUBLICIST

Whether you're aiming for a publicity career in the entertainment business or are simply interested in self-promotion or exposure for your band, the serious pursuit of attention in the world of music commerce requires a variety of skills, both professional and personal. Many of these fall into the realm of journalism and communications: writing, research, organization, and photography. But probably most valuable for the publicist are good verbal communication abilities as well as "people" skills—the ability to interact effectively with a wide assortment of personalities. You'll be dealing with magazine and newspaper editors, radio and TV producers, club owners, photographers, writers, artists, and other musicians, and you'll have to know how to work with these people on their own ground.

Also useful are a healthy sense of competition (needed to put up the good fight in a very competitive industry) and a spirit of tenacity, which means a willingness to stick with a project until the very conclusion, that is, airtime or publication day.

The hunt for exposure also requires flexibility: at various times you'll have to fill the shoes of a journalist, a diplomat, an expert problem-solver, a confidante, a mediator, and an amateur psychologist, among other roles. Being an avid reader—a "media junkie"—is also vital. Let's look more closely at some of these requirements.

KNOW THE HISTORY

If you're a rock musician doing your own publicity, you probably know heaps about pop lore and the entire spectrum of musical influences, from the well known to the obscure. But if you're coming from a management or noncreative perspective, you'll have to become well versed in both the current music scene and its history. If a record-company vice-president or a hot young guitarist mentions Charlie Christian or Duane Allman to you, the names should click right away so you can respond.

This kind of knowledge can be critical at music-business functions. At a party, for example, the young publicist who obviously has never heard of Spike Jones, Etta James, King Sunny Adé, James Blood Ulmer, or the Residents may leave the impression of someone not "in the know," and perhaps not worthy of being taken seriously. The need for a thorough knowledge of pop music is vital for a person who wants to get in, and stay in, the music business.

MUSICAL FLEXIBILITY

"So-and-so's mind is like a steel trap," the old joke goes, "closed." In music PR there are a few things that'll get you into the unemployment line faster, but not many.

You might call it human nature, but it is easy to become locked into one type of music—your favorite—at the exclusion of all others. It's fun to have your own pet style, whether it's head-busting rock, symphonic music, hip-hop, or Christian pop, and everybody has a pet musical idiom. The tendency, quite understandably, is to want to work in the business with your favorite musical type, which is fine—up to a point. The simple fact is that the people with the most staying power in the profession have the willingness and wherewithal to work with many different artists and widely varying styles. The ability to jump musical types is mandatory for any person who's serious about the business, whether they like the music personally or not.

Fans often have a tendency to bad-rap music that doesn't fit their taste. Publicists, however, should avoid this negative trait at all costs, because in the music business—and it's a very cliquish industry—you never know who's listening. The person down the hall may have just produced a soft-pop record and is quite proud of it.

You may hate country music, or rap, or you may think dance music is mindless or folk-pop is wimpy, but keep your mouth shut about it. The blunt truth is that record-company presidents don't care what your favorite music is. As a rule, they have projects in mind constantly and they want the job done correctly—and without the griping that's typical of amateurs.

Of course, if you're working on a do-it-yourself basis and don't have to deal with record-company presidents, then the music you're promoting is probably *only* going to be stuff you like, or perhaps even songs you wrote or arranged. Here musical eclecticism is not strictly required. But for the in-house or self-employed professional publicist, flexibility—both emotional and intellectual—is very important.

KNOW THE MEDIA OUTLETS

Most often, a musical client needs all the exposure he or she can get (exceptions, such as superstar acts, will be covered in Chapter X). So, as a rule, much of the publicist's time is spent researching the possible media outlets for a client and how to get to them.

The publicity person is *always* looking for angles and "hooks" that may make the client more of an exposable commodity. This activity takes numerous forms: thorough research into a band's history, gossip tidbits, and simple human-interest anecdotes. Ideas may come to you at really odd times—sitting in a club, driving, laying in bed staring at the ceiling, watching late-night TV—you name it.

While constantly on the lookout for angles, the pro publicist is also searching for *all* possible outlets, not just the obvious ones like *Musician* or *Vibe*. Other viable targets, often overlooked, include high-school newspapers, college radio, and specialty publications that cover everything from coin collecting to auto racing and women's issues.

While pop-culture and music publications such as *Rolling Stone* and *Spin* are clearly desirable for musical clients, that's only part of the publicist's real horizon. It is deceptively easy to overlook the less obvious or even tangential media outlets. In so doing, lots of valuable exposure may be lost for clients who could really use it—clients such as emerging acts, music groups who are changing artistic courses, acts making a comeback, and many others. Keeping abreast of all music publications and trends will help you avoid missing out on some of those vital "secondary" vehicles for exposure.

It's important for the practicing or beginning publicist (or anyone wanting to get into the music business) to read and then read some more, including all of the pop music press and music industry trade papers. Regular once-overs of all the fan magazines are also necessary. Experience will show you how to scan for items that may be important to your—or your client's—career.

Also, ignore the DJ and touch that dial. This maxim for the music professional holds true in the office, at home, and especially while traveling. You should consistently use the "scan" button in cars and don't let dust gather on other tuners. That radio or TV station you blip across in San Diego or Orlando just may have a locally produced interview show, and may be interested in artists that fit your client roster. Also, the publicist must be aware of developing trends, such as esoteric music specialty shows that can pop up without notice all over the country. Any of these trends may hold a hidden exposure angle that other publicists have overlooked. Also, it's imperative these days to be connected and to know your way around the Internet/Web (more on this in later chapters).

THINK LIKE AN EDITOR

The ability to put yourself in the mind of the information-seeking journalist is an extremely profitable trait for a music PR person. Rather than taking the approach of "I want this," or "I need that," you should be attuned to the types of items or information tidbits that would be attractive or useful to an editor. Approach your artist's career development with an eye on what might appeal to particular outlets: "*Random Notes* might be interested in this," or "*Guitar Player* might want to cover our bassist," are the types of mental connections that you should make.

Accomplishing this means thinking like an editor, constantly looking for what an editor may need. A certain amount of journalistic experience is very helpful in developing this mental edge. Work on a student newspaper, or radio or TV station, is invaluable here. Knowledge of the basics of newswriting, journalism, feature writing, creative writing, and editing is extremely useful. These experiences help the aspiring publicist get into the world of the media firsthand—and that can pay off geometrically in the future.

BE PROFESSIONAL

There are two approaches to looking for publicity: as a professional or as an amateur. The latter, often a person who selfishly thinks of the media only as a source to be exploited, is destined to look for other employment. The pro, on the other hand, who uses professional techniques and tools, can carve a rewarding career and generate immense exposure. The best music PR people are information brokers, and they conduct themselves just like other brokers, whether financial or real estate, treating themselves and their contacts with respect. They, in turn, are respected by even the crustiest investigative journalist.

Getting press clippings delivered by the hand-truck—the proof of exposure—is by no means an impossible feat. Success, as later chapters will show, often boils down to the simplest commonsense considerations. But it also requires a lot of preparation and know-how. Like a master magician, the music publicist knows *all* the tricks of the trade, not 75 percent of them.

THE HISTORY OF MUSIC PR

There's more than a little irony in our use of the term "professional" in much of the previous discussion. It is only in recent years that this word has been applied with any accuracy to the activity of plugging or hyping a musical artist. In the past, the reputation of music PR people has been checkered, to put it politely, and a look at the growth of the music industry will highlight some of the reasons.

The Early Days

While there is very little documentation about the roots of music publicity, the field has been found to date back at least as far as 1900.

In the era of early recording techniques, the sale of sheet music was a very important sector of the music business. During this period, before the dawn of radio in 1922, sheet-music salesmen were called "music pushers," and they often augmented their pitches with live performances on street corners and in music halls. These turn-of-the-century music pitchmen would occasionally call on newspaper and magazine offices hoping to get added exposure for their clients.

Circuses of the period would garner attention with noisy, colorful parades and fireworks displays. According to his "Arts & Entertainment" biography, Harry Houdini, the legendary illusionist and escape artist, was an early master of publicity. In the early 1900s, he would perform free shows on the eve of an appearance. Quite often these were staged outside newspaper offices—and the resulting exposure was a given, a natural. Houdini's water-based stunts were carefully choreographed for the best camera angles.

Howard Bloom, a New York–based author and music PR consultant who has worked extensively with numerous superstar acts such as Prince, John Mellancamp, and ZZ Top, gives a thumbnail sketch of the early years:

> Print media has been changing since the 1920s. Then it was the whole ball of wax.
>
> In 1920, a major national magazine like *Collier's* was the equivalent of what ABC, NBC, and CBS television networks have been over the last couple of years. Those publications were the advertisers' best means to reach a tremendous mass market. Everybody in the country who was anybody and who read the English language read the mass-market periodicals. Those magazines could pay a writer $10,000 for a story. Taking inflation into account, they were paying between $100 and $125,000 for a story. If you were Pepsodent toothpaste or Cadillac, that's where you advertised.
>
> In 1922, a major revolution took place: the introduction of radio. In that year 600 radio stations were licensed in the United States. It had a devastating impact on the print media and on the record industry.
>
> Record industry sales, which had been very strong, dropped 80 percent. If you had been running a record company that was grossing $100,000 a year, you suddenly found yourself grossing $20,000 a year and firing your staff. At the same time, over the course of the following years, print ceased to be king of mass-market media and radio took over.
>
> Radio networks were the big thing. Publicists who had been scrambling to get a mention in *Collier's* were now scrambling to get some sort of mention on the "Jack Benny Show" or on the NBC Radio Network.
>
> Then came 1948 and television, and the situation shifted all over again. The same publicists were now scrambling to get print, radio, and television mentions. In the last few years a couple of other innovations have occurred. Fortunately print never died, nor did radio. Radio syndications became very important. You could do an interview with Mary Turner in L.A. and that interview could appear on 250 different radio stations around the country. Of course, video is very important now—the cable outlets. NBC, ABC, and CBS are no longer going to be the media kingpins that they have been for most of our lifetime because cable is taking away their audience to a large extent.
>
> In 1920, you could have gotten by with being able to deal exclusively with print media. By 1925, you'd have to know how to deal with both radio and print. By 1950, you'd have to know how to deal with radio, print, and television. [Today] you must deal with radio, print, television, cable, and radio syndication. And, of course, there is now the explosion of the new technologies—the Internet/Web and a host of exciting new delivery systems.

Past Methods

In years past, music publicists used a variety of methods to generate added press coverage. Some of these appear quaint today, and some of the basics are still utilized.

During the 1930s and 1940s music publicists shamelessly made up stories that they thought would fit their artists' images. Jazz books of the period make occasional references to press agents as freewheeling hustlers. These tough, clever operators made up the rules as they went along, and they were certainly not above publicity stunts.

In the biography *The Moon's A Balloon,* David Niven told the story of a 1939 PR stunt that backfired. For the New York premiere of *Snow White and the Seven Dwarfs,* Disney Studios hired seven small people to dress in period costume and walk around the roof of the theater. During a delay in the screening, someone passed them up several bottles of whiskey. The group got roaring drunk and paraded above the street—stark naked.

In the early 1950s, the R&B singer Screamin' Jay Hawkins was driven onstage in a Cadillac convertible, lying inside a coffin. During the same period, the pianist Liberace got extra media mileage from his expensive, elaborate outfits.

Paralleling the advent of rock and roll in the 1950s was a proliferation of teen idol and pop-star magazines, which added tons of fodder to the music publicist's mill. Publications like *Hit Parader* were heavily illustrated with photographs and concentrated on hobbies, romances, and exotic lifestyles of the stars.

Then, as rock and roll matured into *rock* in the 1960s, there were sweeping changes in the music, in pop culture itself, and in the media. Several new publications appeared, including *Rolling Stone* and *Crawdaddy,* and they used rock as a mainstay of their content. This was a "boom" period for the record business, with dozens of new stars established and very healthy sales. There were more avenues for exposure, seemingly in every direction, as more publications debuted and thousands of radio stations changed to rock formats.

A plethora of semi-professional and privately published magazines devoted to rock music and its attendant culture cropped up during the late 1960s and early 1970s. Called "fanzines," these publications launched the careers of numerous music writers and critics and provided yet another publicity outlet.

The 1970s saw unprecedented sales increases in the music business. The phenomenon of the multi-million-selling album had arrived, and many in the record industry saw no reason for this ever to change. It was a lavish period in the record industry, full of wasteful practices and enormous profits. One by one, record labels slipped into comfortable, smug habits. Very expensive parties and group airplane junkets were commonplace, for example, and huge promotion/publicity budgets were rarely questioned.

In the late 1970s, if an album release sold poorly, many record labels would simply reservice their entire mailing lists. So it was common for deejays and critics to get two and even three copies of the same LP.

Record-pressing quality levels began to dip, and several companies embarked on a dangerous course: they would release albums that contained a lot of less-than-high-quality material. There were consumer complaints, but few in the business took any notice. The sloppy business practices did not bypass music PR offices. Too often, record labels perceived their PR departments as little more than secretarial positions and paid little attention to the credentials of the people they hired.

During this devil-may-care period, many people seemed to view music PR as an easy entry into the business and a chance to party with the stars. Instead of professionalism, publicists often responded with glib come-ons and shoddy materials. The archetypal "PR hacks" of this period thought nothing of lying to media people and making promises that they couldn't fulfill, or had no intention of keeping. The upshot was a bad reputation, and a lingering one, in the media.

To editors and electronic journalists, the image of the music publicist became one of an untrustworthy parasite, full of hype and little substance. During the late 1970s, one Nashville reporter informed his boss that he was leaving the newspaper to become a music press agent. "I'd rather see you become a pimp," the editor snorted in disgust.

The Crash of 1979

Even though music critics from coast to coast decried the sorry state of the industry, these practices persisted to the end of the decade. Then, in the summer of 1979, the inevitable happened. With stunning speed, a depression hit the music business from top to bottom and sales fell dramatically. Record buyers had simply had enough. There were drastic layoffs at several labels, and artist rosters were trimmed. The record business shrank and then shrank some more through the dawn of the 1980s.

As the music business struggled back to health, the industry began to take on a very different profile. It was leaner, much more cost-conscious, and more businesslike. During the shrinkage of 1979–80, unqualified people—and those with poor reputations—were swept away like chaff.

In their place has come a kind of new breed of music-business professional, better educated and with much-improved business acumen. Today, the successful music publicist is vastly different from his or her counterpart of just two decades ago. The music PR person is now more qualified, more able to respond quickly to ever-shifting situations, and better equipped to deal with the competition for media attention. The result is a new respect for the field, making the publicist's task of working with the media a whole lot easier.

PART 2

BASIC TOOLS: THE PRESS KIT

4

PRESS KIT
COMPONENTS

Like a surgeon or a computer graphics artist, the contemporary music publicist relies heavily on an array of specialized tools. These devices, and the information that goes along with them, are the real foundations of a successful publicity campaign.

The quality of the materials you send out is an accurate indicator of the professional caliber behind them. These materials also have a direct reflection on how the client is perceived, so it's extremely important to go for the best that are possible.

Some of the items in the music press agent's velvet tool box are venerable, tested, and proven true over several generations. Others are quite new—the spawn of an electronic era. Regardless of their age, each of these performs a specific function, and they all help in the PR person's never-ending challenge: reaching out, engaging, informing, and generating exposure. The following devices also have the beauty of flexibility. Properly prepared and fine-tuned, they can work equally well for an outrageous rock band, a "heat-seeking" engineer, a label president, a reclusive songwriter, or a chamber ensemble.

THE COMPONENTS

The basic "outgoing" tools are the press kit (or media pak), the pitch letter, the press release, the fact sheet, the video bio, and the public-service announcement (PSA). On the internal or office side, the most often used tools include the media list, media guides, the gig sheet, the telephone, a personal computer (or terminal) with related devices (including CD-ROM, printer, and sound), a TV/VCR combo, and the facsimile (fax) machine. The telephone, related communications skills, and electronic hardware/software will be covered in separate sections.

The Most Important Device

A remarkable multifunctional tool, the press kit is the heart of any client's media campaign. It's both a media-information tool and an ambassador—it goes many,

SPIN

roots radical

BujuB
is bringin
Bob Mar
back int
crazed
Elena
catch

[illegible body column text]

FOR IMMEDIATE RELEASE

PU

AP

THE CHAMPION RETU

BUJU BANTON DROPS NEW SINGLE "CHAM
LOOSE CANNON DEBUT 'TIL SHILOH TO BE

Reggae superstar Buju Banton has returned with 'TIL SHILO
Cannon Records. To be released July 18, the follow-up to hi
JAMAICA is set to break musical boundaries by bridging th
Marley and the sound of contemporary dancehall. 'TIL SH
pulsating "Champion," will hit the streets

Buju Banto
premier mu
in one year
America, w

Leading the
Rob "Fonks
"Champagne"
included on t
according to E
graphic sexuali
and self-respect
friends and so
Stories, a poign
commodity/In
ever play." Othe
"Til I'm Laid to
legendary soundi
and Buju Banton
Garnett Silk ("Co
boasts background

A reflection of his

1973
- Born Mark Anthony
  13 sisters and one d
  African slaves brou
  slavery. Grew up
  child, gets the nick

1985 - 12 years old
- Takes nickname a
  artists, Burro Ban

- Worked initially
  song called "I

- During this time
  producer to pro
  for all rights to
  artist trying to
  Rambo Interna

1987
- He recorded

1988 - 15 years old
- Recorded tra
  including th

1989
- Meets Dave
  His first tw

1990
- Although
  market p
  producer
  and "Bri

Loose Cane

This fairly basic press kit, produced for reggae artist Buju Banton, includes a publicity photo, a biography in a time-line format, a set of press clips, album information, a promotional decal, and a CD. A press kit can be more or less elaborate depending on the money available and the inclination of the record label.

many places where the PR person cannot (or doesn't have time to go) and it makes a critical impression.

Besides its extremely important media function, the press kit also has duties in other areas. For a new band, it may be sent to club owners or prospective booking agents and/or managers. In the case of an established group, the press kit may wind up on numerous desks besides those of editors. These can include corporate executives who may be thinking about sponsoring the group on tour; touring agents or festival officials in other countries; and also people in government (who may be considering the act for a political fundraiser, for example).

Regardless of its destination, the press kit informs the reader about the client—quickly, accurately, and in an interesting manner. It draws the reader in, and gives both a thumbnail sketch and an overall impression of the client. The press kit must get in and accomplish this swiftly and efficiently, because most often the recipient's time is both valuable and limited. It may be a cliché, but the old axiom "the first impression is the most important" is critical in publicity, and is the reason that so much energy is expended on professional press kits.

A high-quality press kit, coupled with professional-level demo materials, can make the difference between an act being dismissed as "just another damn band" and being viewed as "hmm . . . interesting; looks like something we should pursue. . . ." Needless to say, many stacks of dollars may ride on that perception.

Every professional press kit has certain basic components, each with specific uses:

• The jacket, or "cover"

• An artist's biography, or "bio"

• A fact sheet

• One or more photographs

• Article reprints, or "tearsheets"

Press kits are normally accompanied by a cover or "pitch" letter. Nowadays they are also often augmented with a "video bio," a videocassette with interview segments and live performance footage. Depending on the destination, a CD or stereo cassette may also be enclosed.

TIME, MONEY, AND CARE

In the past, some band leaders, managers, and record-label people have put PR materials at the bottom of the priority list. Yet history shows that this is almost always a mistake. In reality, PR materials are just as important as any other factor in the act's career—and that includes the equipment truck, new instruments, and costumes. One veteran publicist puts it this way: "If you have a vintage 1957 Gibson Les Paul that needs restoring, you're not going to give it to an amateur.

You're going to take it to an instrument master. Well, treat the PR materials with the same care." If you follow that advice, in the context of today's entertainment industry, you and your client will be well down the road to a complete career-development package.

Although it's easy to do, it is not always necessary to spend lavish amounts of money to put together a tasteful and effective press kit. The following chapters will show you what to look for if outside professionals are going to handle the preparations. And if you plan to create the materials yourself, the next chapters will step you through the essentials. Read these sections carefully, even if you're hiring out the work. That way you will know if quality work is being delivered, and, if not, you'll be in a position to order revisions and additions to suit your client.

5

THE JACKET

T he jacket is an excellent place to start if you're assembling a press kit from scratch. In a media sense, the cover of the press kit is the sexy costume in which your client goes onstage. It's the part of the kit that gives the crucial first impression.

A type of binder and protector, the jacket holds all the other materials and keeps them organized. It's most often constructed of heavy paper stock and, similar to a school report cover, it has one or two inner sleeves to hold the other materials.

A practical note here: on some paper jackets, the inner sleeves are simply folded over, which leaves them open at the ends. This method, although cheaper, can allow materials to fall out if the jacket is held sideways. This is a real inconvenience in hectic media offices and it can result in materials getting lost—a possibly disastrous event. An editor won't run a photo of your group if it fell on the floor and got trashed. So, if budget permits, use a jacket whose sleeves are sealed at the ends. It's much safer and more efficient.

JACKET ARTWORK

Logos, photos, and other artwork are often included in a jacket's design. This can range from beautifully done images on glossy stock, incorporating the band's logo and the new CD, record, or tape title, to a simple, budget-conscious design with just the band's name. The latter type can be used for more than one record release and is often employed by new acts.

Uniformity is the most important aspect of jacket design—consistency between the record/CD jacket appearance and the PR materials "pak." A striking CD package accompanied by a cheap-looking media kit indicates that the act is "really not there yet" and not to be taken seriously.

On the other hand, a press-kit jacket that is eye-catching and appealing on a certain level—whether bizarre, violent, grotesque, lovely, or some artistic combination thereof—communicates clearly that this act has arrived and has some-

This relatively inexpensive but effective press kit jacket makes use of the silhouetted art logo of R&B trio Skindeep as the focus of its front cover. The back cover uses the black-and-white logo of Loose Cannon, the group's record label.

thing to say. This is an extremely important concept in music publicity, regardless of the act's musical style (or the nonartist client's business philosophy).

If possible, a graphic artist with musical experience should be consulted in the planning stage for a media kit. Most record labels have artists either in house or on retainer. Independent productions, though, may have severe budget restrictions, but there are ways to get around them:

1. Seek out art students in the art department of the nearest college. It may not be too difficult to locate a talented student who is willing to work for modest bucks.

2. Keep the design simple. It's quite possible to get your client's message across without terribly fancy artwork. Put on the old thinking cap, try to consult with knowledgeable people, and decide what's tasteful (if applicable), striking, and evocative. The answer for an engineer's press kit, for example, may be an image generated on a personal computer. For a blues-rock band you might use an old photo from a photographer's collection.

PRINTING

It's a good idea to get several bids or estimates from different printing houses. Ask the artist for advice on reputable printers. Also, since paper is very expensive, carefully consider the number of jackets that will be necessary before their design is obsolete. One guideline might be 50 to 100 for a small regional campaign with a new band and 1,000 for a much larger national campaign with a platinum act.

SIZE

It's wise to stay with a standard-size jacket (9 x 12 inches), and the same goes for the materials inside. If you try to get too weird with these materials—grossly outsized, as some labels have done in the past—they may not fit in filing cabinets. In this case, an editor may just trash the whole package. Be creative elsewhere.

It's quite possible, though, to explore certain innovative designs successfully, but keep the editor's office space in mind—the press kit package may prove useful months down the road. One example of a different design is a clear plastic jacket that shows off a reduced-size poster inside.

6

THE ARTIST'S BIO

The artist's bio is the central nervous system of the press kit. It's the most important item in the media pak and it has the most far-reaching duties. Besides playing a key role on the journalistic side, the bio is also useful in making a mental impression and summing up the act to several parties, each of whom can have a profound impact on the artist's career. These may include prospective managers, financial backers, tour organizers, record labels, film and TV producers, and radio personnel.

The artist's bio is often compared to an entry in an encyclopedia. It must quickly and efficiently educate the reader, who often knows nothing about the artist, and it has to do so in an interesting manner. The artist's bio must also be careful to avoid several pitfalls: it can't be trite or superfluous, or run on to no real end.

The contemporary professional bio has to be loaded with facts and give an accurate, overall picture of the artist or group or other client. While delivering these facts, it must also carve out a psychological image of the artist, showing off the talent, the type of musical expression, and, in capsule form, establish what the artist has to say—musically, socially, and spiritually—in whatever terms that are applicable. In other words, the bio sets up the client with the very best artistic foot forward.

This biographical "short feature story" can, of course, paint widely differing pictures. If the subject is a loud, angry, outrageous rock band, then why? Or if the topic is a shy, petite folksinger, then what is the basis of the personality? The focal point may be an engineer or producer with a recent smash on his or her hands. If so, then what is the subject's technical point of view and how, summarized, was he or she able to achieve that unique sound on the CD?

The text should have the cohesiveness of a short story, with movement and with a definite beginning, middle, and end. It's a professional tool in which every word counts and every paragraph should be studiously edited. The reason for all this painstaking work is that you never know on whose desk it may wind up, and the bio just might make a slim difference in getting a record deal, a major tour, a big radio "add," or other career boost.

MEDIA USES

The bio's primary role is a journalistic one. In this capacity, it works on multiple levels. It must *attract interest,* and it must *inform.* The media pak, proudly holding the bio, is often sent out to numerous media locations either with, or in advance of, the recorded product. The mailing may also coincide with an upcoming tour.

In this case, the bio's first duty is to interest a newspaper entertainment writer, magazine editor, TV producer, radio talk-show coordinator, or several other similar entities. Here's where it's very important that the bio read clearly, contain lots of information, and be presented in an interesting, straightforward style.

One of the golden rules of music publicity (applicable to all promotional materials) is that media people's time is limited, valuable, and often hectic. They don't have time for unnecessary prose or pretentious hype. Keep in mind that any media person is continually flooded with similar materials of varying quality, and this makes for a high level of cynicism among entertainment journalists.

The decision to use, or not to use, the act in question may be made in a matter of moments, and the bio can have a tremendous impact one way or the other. The recorded material (if the journalist listens to it at all) makes a musical statement, and the bio makes a written statement. Ideally, the two should go hand in hand, complementing each other—and hooking the interest of the journalist.

Once the decision has been made to use the artist in a talk show, feature story, or newspaper column, the bio shifts into another function. At this stage it has to brief the writer or host so that he or she can begin to prepare intelligent questions during the upcoming interview.

In some cases the act may not be available for an interview (a foreign band, for instance), or an article may be in the works in a country 7,000 miles away and it's not economically feasible to set up a personal meeting with the artist. For this reason the bio may be the primary source of information for media use. Quite often quotes, anecdotes, and other information in the bio are lifted directly into wire-service copy, record reviews, TV clips, and other media coverage. In fact, the *entire* bio may be used as a feature story by smaller newspapers who are short-staffed and in desperate need of copy. This happens often in a big national campaign.

Bios are also very useful to journalists in the closing stages of story preparation. Once a draft is written, a professional writer will go back to the bio and check all the pertinent facts against those in the manuscript. At most national magazines, an editor will back up the writer and do the same thing.

So there are numerous reasons for the bio to be well-researched and prepared.

The better it reads, and the more informative, then the more it's going to be used, possibly from Paris to Chicago to Tokyo.

Consultant Howard Bloom has this to say about to bio writing:

> We've always tried to be as factual as possible with artist's bios for any of our clients. We operate according to Strunk's book on style. [W. Strunk, Jr., and E.B. White, *The Elements of Style*, Macmillan, 1995.] We avoid adjectives. Most press releases and bios are loaded with adjectives. They will say, "So and so is the most innovative act in the history of rock and roll. His great style is filled with brilliantly imaginative touches." Et cetera.
>
> It will just be one garbage adjective after another with very little to support it. Press people know that it's just nonsense. We like to rely on facts to make our points for us.

PREPARING THE ARTIST'S BIO

Whenever possible, an artist's bio should be prepared by a professional writer, and preferably one with expertise in the field of entertainment. Ask for references and examples of previous work. To locate an experienced bio writer you might try contacting a record-label branch office, the managing editor of a local magazine, or the entertainment editor of a local paper. If the budget is slim, seek out a nearby journalism school or English department and ask for an outstanding student writer. (Students—a vastly underutilized resource—need the money and the experience, and often do a very competent job.)

But sometimes you have to face fiscal reality. If there's no budget to hire out the project, don't despair. Preparing an artist's bio is far from an impossible task, and you needn't be a great writer to compose a workable one. What you do need are some basic journalistic skills and enough time to devote to the preparation. If you're a one-person company—and new at the game—don't panic. You can do it. With the information that follows, you'll be able to write a good, workable bio, and quite likely it'll be better than many done by high-powered agencies.

If you're stuck with the job and have a pathological fear of writing, seek out a friend who may be better able to handle it. If you make a few calls or ask a few people around the local music community, someone will turn up. Work on the bio as a co-produced project. It's nothing to fear; just keep it simple and straightforward. Also, if you're writing a bio for the first time, study existing examples, especially those from major labels. Take a look at formats and use them as a basic frame of reference.

Whether you or an outside professional will prepare the document, three basic steps should be followed: (1) research, (2) interview, and (3) preparation.

The Research Phase

Initially the writer should dig deeply into the act's background and become as familiar with it as humanly possible. Listen to all the recorded product, if any, including the very oldest demos (especially important for a new group; not so much for an established band). If the act has several LPs under its belt, listen carefully and take notes on all the tracks—you never know when a theme or a kind of group personality may emerge.

Get your hands on all written material about the group. The newer the act, the more important this is. If the client is a platinum group or beyond, the "clip file" (library of articles) may be massive, so you can be more selective. Look for articles in the most authoritative publications, such as *Rolling Stone, Vibe, Musician,* or the major metro daily newspapers.

Locate copies of all old bios, if any exist. These can be very informative and save you lots of time in mastering the basic facts about the client.

For established acts, review all existing video material, including music videos, documentaries, news footage, and live concert time. Be persistent; record label and/or management hirelings may be lazy and not want to bother digging through musty archives, but this is important. In the research stage, you don't know when you may stumble across an anecdote, quote, or passage that may be very useful in the actual bio. For the writer, it's better to have far too much material than to have too little.

The Interview Phase

Next, interview the group members (or solo artist, or executive) and do this as thoroughly as possible. Ideally, the interviews should take place in more than one geographic location and time. You'll end up with a better picture of the client this way. This should coincide with seeing the act live (if applicable) or at least reviewing video material.

If it's not geographically possible to get together with the client, try to arrange communication by whatever media is available—phone, mail, E-mail, or fax.

The writer should have a list of questions ready for the client, but don't be afraid to deviate from them. Let the conversation wander if the interviewee seems to want it to. This will often relax the person so that he or she will open up and talk more freely. Some people, especially those unaccustomed to being interviewed, are very nervous about the process and may tend to clam up or give short or sketchy answers.

Keep paying attention and taking at least mental notes, even after the interview is over. Sometimes, when people feel that "the heat is off," they'll inadvertently relax and let go with wonderful anecdotes or usable quotes. Some of the best bio material has been gathered in this fashion, after hours.

The following is a shopping list of basic topics that should be covered in an interview.

For a musical client:

- Hometown of the artist

- Date and circumstances of a group's formation

- Information about previous or formative bands

- Education or any formal musical training of members (including awards and other achievements)

- Anecdotes: interesting tidbits about touring, recording, the band's activities—anything that gives personality to the act

- Stories behind the new songs: what inspired them, where they were written, unusual aspects of the recording process

- Capsule information on each new song: what it's about (even in the vaguest terms) or some kind of description, whether it's girl-meets-boy, "let's go out and party," cruising on the highway, or a topic with political relevance or related to a social cause

- Musical category or style of the artist. This is often difficult for bands to describe, but it must be done. Work with the members until a term or phrase, no matter how esoteric, is acceptable to them: heavy metal, experimental rock, dance music, folk, electronic chamber music, jazz, or whatever. It's okay to coin a new phrase as long as it clearly sums up the act's musical personality. (If the musical genre is not clear in the bio, then you run the risk of a journalist pigeonholing the group, perhaps quite incorrectly.)

For a technical client (such as a producer or engineer):

- Basic biographical questions: hometown, and so on

- Technical education (including self-training), and membership in technical or professional societies

- Career highlights (the first big project or first time with a great new piece of equipment, for example)

- Philosophy on technology in his or her field

- Roster of acts or other clients worked with

- Technical innovations or equipment he or she developed

- Personal sources of ideas for projects

- Future projects

- New equipment or other breakthroughs this person is anticipating (new "toys" for the engineer, for example)

For a corporate client
(industry executive, consultant, manager, or concert promoter):

- Basic biographical and education questions, as above

- Professional background: positions held (including college internships and entry-level jobs)

- Philosophy, outlook on current position, plans for the company or for future expansion

- Personal view of the industry today (current debates, legal situations, exciting developments, potential crises)

- Viewpoints on developing trends in the entertainment business (related to the personal view question above, but more specific)

Interview Tips

Take extensive notes during all interviews with the client. Also tape-record conversations whenever possible. Keep a pen and small notebook handy at all times, even in the darkest, loudest clubs—you never know when a client will remember something important or utter something funny or enlightening about the act.

Be on the lookout constantly for even small things that help give the act a persona. These can come from seemingly unlikely places at times: stage antics or unusual aspects of the live show; rare instruments that are used; something said by a fan or audience member. Remember, you are trying to assemble a total picture of the group.

For the sake of professionalism, avoid the typical pitfalls of research. Don't let tools and materials—tape recorders, notebooks, pocketbooks, and so on—out of your sight. Having a wonderful interview stolen, along with your tape machine, while you're at the bar, is an indescribably frustrating experience. Also, band members hate to redo interviews. Tip: Invest in a second machine, perhaps a microcassette recorder, and run both machines simultaneously—all the real pros do this for safety.

THE PREPARATION PHASE

Once the research is finished and the interview is complete, you're ready to enter the preparatory phase. For this task it's a good idea to seek out a location, office or otherwise, that is quiet and free of interruptions.

Useful equipment other than basic pencil and paper includes a personal computer with word-processing software, one or more legal pads, some ballpoint or felt-tip pens, and a tape recorder with an on/off foot control (quite inexpensive and very handy). An optional but very helpful tool is a dry-erase board (similar to a blackboard, but you write on it with an erasable felt marker), which is quite useful for organizing materials and creating the outline: you can stand back and see the whole plan at a glance. Many novelists, screenwriters, and ad copywriters use these in conjunction with PCs.

Carefully review the magazine and newspaper articles and bios that you collected earlier. As you read, underline or highlight any areas that strike you as important. Trust your first impressions; you can finalize any decisions later in the outline phase.

As you read, keep a running table of notes on a legal pad. Fragmentary entries are fine; you just need something to jog your memory, such as "started as garage band, broke in three months." You'll be surprised at how quickly an overall picture of the client begins to emerge. Look for recurring phrases or descriptions through the various articles and old bios. "Prolific songwriter," "often compared to . . . ," "fluid guitar style," "outrageous behavior shocked audiences" are the types of phrases you may come across. These recurrent little tidbits may be signs pointing to key passages in the new bio that you're writing.

Then it's time to transcribe the interview tapes. (A word processor is wonderful here because it can handle the information faster than you can type it in—and you don't have to hit "return" at the end of each line.)

Depending on your experience or preference, listen to a snippet of conversation, then halt the machine and type it in. Some writers hire out the transcription process, which is fine if you're extremely busy. However, the actual line-by-line transcribing is an excellent way to become more familiar with the client in a hurry. As the work goes along, don't hesitate to stop and make quick notes, either in the draft, in a separate computer "window," or on the legal pad.

It is not necessary to transcribe the entire interview verbatim. In most instances you'll only need to enter the core of the conversation. Exceptions are very technical sections and passages that are full of good quotes. Normally, these jump out at you as you listen and type: "When she sang the fourth take, the hair stood up on the nape of my neck."

The Six-Step Outline

After all notation and transcription is finished, it's time to create the outline, the roadmap that will guide you home to an effective bio. It's a good idea to start with a very simple, generalized format—just hit the real high spots first and then fill in the details. There are several approaches you can use, but we'll cover a basic, workable formula.

The purpose of this outline is to have the finished draft read tightly, proceed in a logical manner, and keep the interesting things zipping along sentence by sentence. Also, some clients' stories are very complicated, full of twists, and interviews may contain indelicate passages that you must politely skip over. This step-by-step approach will help you sort through these problems, even for a veteran eight-album platinum act that's had its share of musical direction changes, divorces, flops, overdoses, fights, smash hits, and other niceties common in pop music. Here's the basic outline:

1. *Introductory Statement.* Here, you introduce the client and quickly establish the persona, whether musical, technical, or corporate. Rely heavily on facts and keep adjectives/adverbs to a minimum.

2. *Current Summary.* This is a capsule of the client's activity at the present and gets the reader rapidly into the new CD release, tour, film, or other product. The same applies to nonartist entertainment clients: present their studio or label position and latest project. You don't have to tell the whole story here, just the highlights.

3. *Additional Information.* Stretch out in this passage, within reason, with some key points that you've isolated. A good rule is one to four paragraphs, depending on the client's career history. For a new act, this section may be rather short. A multiplatinum band or heavyweight producer would rate more detail.

4. *History and Formation.* Often overlooked by amateur writers, this is an equally vital section that will be drawn upon heavily by editors, writers, and electronic media people alike. For musical acts, include the locale and circumstances of the group's formation or soloist's development. Include funny or unusual anecdotes; just about everyone has them. Musical influences are good to mention here, and they help to nail down the client's musical persona. For technical/corporate clients, go into some detail about education and early experience.

5. *Elaboration: New Release, Tour, or Tech/Corporate Activities.* This is an information "grab bag" about the client, and it's deliberately placed near the end. Readers who are truly interested will get this far. An assignment editor, for example, will have already made a yes or no decision. Writers will refer to this section as they work on an article, and often they'll rely on it heavily. Here's where you should elaborate slightly on key points that are not in the first passage, such as a client's artistic, technical, or business philosophy. This is also the place for interesting tidbits about the new record, equipment, or details of a new tour. If the client is a studio, you might provide a walk-through description.

6. *Summary/Closing.* As in a good feature story, the final passage brings the reader to a satisfying conclusion. Look through your notes for a quote that has a kind of summary feel to it, then build up to it. A good example may be a band's philosophy: "We want the audience to have as much fun as we're having onstage." For a tech or business client, you can use future goals or professional plans.

One way to put this outline to use is to set up a chart that incorporates specific data about your artist. The following is a professional, virtually foolproof diagram that takes a three-tiered form. The left column presents the *main outline;* the center holds the *key points;* and the right column is an entry area for *best quotes.* This format can be used on a computer monitor, an idea board, or a legal pad.

OUTLINE	KEY POINTS	QUOTES
1. Intro Statement	New CD; musically different	"Change to other instruments"
2. Current Summary	Basic tracks recorded in home studio	"Time to challenge the audience"
3. Additional Information	Use acoustic and unusual instruments	"Guest vocal was really hoarse"
4. History and Formation	Guest vocal by Tinsley Ellis	"Not only unusual but makes them think"
5. Elaboration	"Angel Tears" inspired by old tombstone	"Tinsley used a rare eight-string guitar"
6. Summary/Closing		"Always looking for new ideas"

Draft Setup

Now it's time to prepare a draft of the bio. Center the heading at the top of page one. Depending on your client, the heading may read "Artist Biography," "Corporate Profile," "Technical Profile," or whatever else is suitable. Another option is simply to use "BIO."

If the client is an individual—a solo artist or record label president—center the person's name at the top of the text, two lines below the heading. For a musical act that has more than one member, list each member and their instrument(s) in a centered area at the top, below the heading.

There's no single perfect way to begin writing. Every writer confronts the blank page or screen differently. The main point is: do something. If your method is to knock out a very sketchy, ragged first draft, that's fine. If you can't sleep until you have a fairly tight introductory passage, that's equally okay.

Keep an eye on the outline, but don't let it dominate you. If you find the draft varying a little, don't worry about it; sometimes a phrase will just seem to fit and it's best to go with it. This is especially important in the rough-draft stage when you want to keep moving through the text.

Don't worry too much about sentence structure, punctuation, or any other details of grammar at this stage. The central point here is that it's much easier to work from some kind of draft, no matter how much it resembles Cyrillic, than it is to create a perfect bio out of thin air.

Once the first draft is in some kind of form, no matter how rough, the next step is to start polishing or fine-tuning it. Many writers who work on a computer like to print out a hard copy of this initial effort; seeing how it looks on paper helps

DAVE ALVIN

My name is Dave Alvin and I've just recorded my first live solo album, *INTERSTATE CITY*, at the fabulous Continental Club in Austin, Texas. For the past three years, since the release of my CD, *MUSEUM OF HEART*, I've been touring the bars and nightclubs along the great American interstate highway system in rented or borrowed vans and cars. Sometimes I toured with just my acoustic guitar but mainly I was with my blues/folk/rock/R&B band, THE GUILTY MEN.

One of the reasons I chose to record a live album was because there were nights on stage when The Guilty Men blew me away with how good they are. These guys are as good as anyone I've ever worked with and I've been a member of some pretty good bands (The Blasters, X, The Knitters) and I've worked and recorded with some pretty good people (Tom Waits, Bob Dylan, Syd Straw, The Iguanas, Big Joe Turner, Sonny Burgess.) The Guilty Men consistently make me proud to be on stage with them.

Steel guitarist GREG LEISZ, who produced my last CD, *KING OF CALIFORNIA*, has been playing with me since my first solo album, *ROMEO'S ESCAPE*, in 1987. He's now one of the most in demand studio musicians anywhere, recording with k.d. lang, Gillian Welch, Jimmie Dale Gilmore, Matthew Sweet, Smashing Pumpkins, Joni Mitchell, Victoria Williams, Eddie Floyd, and Rosie Flores to name a few. Drummer BOBBY LLOYD HICKS is a member of the legendary Midwest band The Skeletons and has recorded and toured with Steve Forbert, Jonathan Richman, Syd Straw, Martha Reeves and, uh, Boxcar Willie. Bobby is also one of the most soulful singers around. I've known bassist GREGORY BOAZ since the old L.A. punk rock scene in the early eighties when he played with the hard edged Tex & The Horseheads. He has since become a rock solid blues bassman playing with Mick Taylor, Hook Hererra, Juke Logan, and blues chanteuse, Brenda Burns. Pianist RICK SOLEM plays like his fingers are haunted by the ghosts of boogie woogie powerhouse Pete Johnson, country rocker Moon Mullican, New Orleans genius Professor Longhair, and sometimes even Thelonius Monk. Rick is so good, he scares the hell out of me. As you can imagine, THE GUILTY MEN have no problem following me whether I feel like playing blues, country, rock and roll or folk ballads (It's all the same to me anyway). By the way, I'd like to thank *INTERSTATE CITY* special guests: Austin harmonica wizard TED RODDY and Forth Worth's country/soul queen KATY MOFFATT.

Another reason I wanted to do a live CD is that after the release of the mainly acoustic *KING OF CALIFORNIA*, I've noticed a split in my audience between people who want to hear my lyrics and those who want to see me sweat and bash on a loud guitar. Since my next studio recording will be in the quieter style, I wanted to do something for my rocking fans.

HIGHTONE RECORDS
220 4th STREET #101 • OAKLAND, CALIFORNIA 94607 • TELEPHONE (510) 763-8500
FAX (510) 763-8558

Some of the songs, like "Long White Cadillac," " Thirty Dollar Room," " Romeo's Escape," "Dry River"and the " Jubilee Train/Do Re Mi/Promised Land" medley, have been live favorites for a long time. Other songs, like" Interstate City," " Out In California" and "Mister Lee" (a tribute to a man I've known since I was a kid, who taught me as much about life as he did about music, the great New Orleans saxaphonist LEE ALLEN) are newer. "Waiting For The Hard Times To Go" was written by the late and under-recognized California songwriter/singer JIM RINGER. Almost all the songs are "road" songs in that they're about people in motel rooms and barrooms, on highways and interstates and street corners, a long way from whatever homes they left behind, looking for something they lost or never had to begin with.

During the short breaks in the endless touring I managed to record *KING OF CALIFORNIA* as well as produce two CDs for BIG SANDY & HIS FLY-RITE BOYS and CDs for THE DERAILERS, TOM RUSSELL, CHRIS GAFFNEY, THE FORBIDDEN PIGS and co-produce, with TOM RUSSELL, *TULARE DUST, A Songwriters' Tribute To Merle Haggard*. I also put out a book of prose poems titled, *ANY ROUGH TIMES ARE NOW BEHIND YOU* (Incommunicado Press). Occasionally I also managed to sleep.

It sometimes seems like a long time since my brother, Phil, and I formed THE BLASTERS in our hometown of Downey, California in 1979. We just wanted to play the music we'd grown up listening to (country blues, city blues, rhythm and blues, honky tonk, rockabilly, hillbilly, folk singers, protest singers, gospel singers and surf guitar slingers) and hopefully be able to quit our day jobs and still be able to pay the rent. I haven't been a fry cook in a long time.

I hope you'll enjoy *INTERSTATE CITY* and I'll see you down the road.

Publicity : Mark Pucci Media   404 - 816 -7393

This bio of established singer/songwriter Dave Alvin ignores the usual hyperbole of press releases and allows the artist to write his own biography, which both touches on his musical history and promotes his latest album.

in the editing process. Print the rough draft out in double-spaced form to allow for editing marks between lines.

If you're working on a personal computer, make several backup copies of the draft, on more than one disk. Before 1980, the dog might have chewed the draft into bits. Since then, many a writer (including this one) has, in a haze of fatigue, mistakenly destroyed the only existing draft onscreen. Static electricity and dirty or temperamental disk drives can also factor in this equation.

At this stage, a great editing trick is to have a second person read the draft aloud. It's an excellent way to spot flaws in the work and give a clearer idea of how to fix it. Some writers elect to write a second, tighter draft before the verbal session.

As you listen, take notes. These will help a lot in smoothing the draft. Be on the lookout for sentences that are too long. (As a rule, more than twenty words puts you in the danger zone.)

Tips on Style and Format

When style questions arise, it's best to consult a good style manual such as *The AP Style Book, The New York Times Manual of Style and Usage,* or Nicholas P. Criscuolo's *Look It Up!* In the meantime, keep in mind some of the following suggestions when you're dealing with bio preparation.

- At all costs, avoid overblown adjectives and adverbs—they immediately destroy credibility. "Phenomenal," "incredible," and the like shouldn't be used unless they are absolutely true (and this is quite rare). And if you do use terms like this to push across a mediocre act, people will see through it right away.

- Avoid exclamation marks. They shriek overstatement and give any manuscript an amateurish tone.

- Use quotes to drive home key points. At the same time, however, don't "coast" on quotes. Select the best three or four for the bio. Paraphrase everything else.

- Don't feel compelled to tell the entire story in the bio. It's usually impossible. Also, keep in mind the "encyclopedia entry" idea: just include the high points. The other information will come out in live interviews with the client.

- Be certain that a contact name and phone number, fax, e-mail address and Web (URL) address is included on page one, upper right-hand corner. This is vital, in case a writer needs more information. For example:

> Contact: Jane Rock
> (agency name optional)
> 212-000-1111
> Fax: 212-000-1212
> Web: jrock@www.com

- Follow journalism style in keeping paragraphs comparatively short, averaging four to five sentences.

- Line spacing in the final draft can be either double-spaced, space-and-a-half, or single-spaced.

- A good overall layout is 1½ inches for the top margin, 1 inch for the bottom margin, and 65 characters per line.

- Underline album/CD titles, and the titles of books, films, and plays. Titles of singles are set off with quotation marks. If you have the printing capability, you can swap italics for underlining.

- Aim for a maximum length of two pages, unless the client is a megaplatinum act that's been around for ten years. In that case, hold it to four pages of predominantly current information. (Lots of their history will already be available in music reference books.) Some labels have recently gone to a format of using copy on both sides of the page to save money.

- Remember, this is not literature. Avoid the urge to get cute with strong language—no matter how outrageous or profane the client is. Avoid the deadly four-letter words and stay with mild invective (heck, butt, and the like). Some editors can be quite conservative, and, if offended, can zap your act. Establish the client's persona in a more creative way.

- Indicate the end with —30— or ###, and center the symbols.

- Bios of more than one page should be stapled, with each page numbered.

- Choose a white or near-white paper color. Use a type style that is rather bold and easy to read. The bio may be photocopied and/or transmitted over fax machines, and you don't want the images to degrade so badly that they're hard to read.

- 20-lb. paper stock is fine, unless you want to go fancier with a really successful client. Plain white copy paper is okay if you're on a tight budget, trying to break a new act.

The Final Draft

As the draft nears completion, it should read tightly and move forward with a rhythm you can sense when it's read aloud. If possible, have a computer spell-checker access the draft, but beware of letting the spell-checker do all the work—though it will catch actual misspellings, it may not alert you to words that are spelled correctly but are not what you intended ("it's" instead of "its," for example, or "there" instead of "their"). Whether or not you use a spell-checker, you should still have at least one other person look over the draft carefully to spot spelling, punctuation, and other bloopers. Even the best writers get "forest-and-

are one of the blues' greatest success stories of the 1990s. In the span of just six short years and five albums, they have gone from virtual obscurity to become one of the most popular acoustic blues groups in the world. There are, of course, many reasons for their success. *Ms.* magazine, however, summed it up best, "Recipe for success: start with three talented musicians. Stir in rich melodies, honky-tonk rhythms, and spicy-hot lyrics. Then add a bucketful of courage, the kind it takes to leave home and career in mid-life. Simmer for a few years in smoky road-houses and cheap motels. The result? Saffire—The Uppity Blues Women."

And now the story continues. Saffire—The Uppity Blues Women's new Alligator album, *Cleaning House* (AL 4840), finds Ann Rabson (piano/guitar/vocals), Gaye Adegbalola (guitar/harmonica/ vocals) and Andra Faye McIntosh (bass/guitar/mandolin/fiddle/vocals) singing and playing their unique brand of sassy, witty, and fiercely independent music with spirit and soul. *Cleaning House* mixes acoustic guitar, piano, upright bass, harmonica, mandolin, fiddle and soulful, harmonizing vocals with contemporary, slice-of-life lyrics, all from a decidedly female point of view. Originality abounds on the album, with six songs by Gaye and three by Ann. And the songs they didn't write receive the Saffire treatment, rendering each song their very own.

From the propulsive *Rocket Ship* to the sultry *(I'll Be Your) Sweet Black Angel*, to the philosophical dance song, *Tomorrow Ain't Promised*, to the humorous advice of *If Love Hurts (You're Not Doing It Right)*, the interplay of vocal harmonies, boogie-woogie piano, passionate guitar, smokey harmonica, spicy fiddle, bass and mandolin

makes *Cleaning House* Saffire's most original and fully realized album. The carefully chosen covers, including Rick Estrin's *Don't Do It* and Johnny Copeland's *Nobody But You*, not to mention Marshall Chapman's *Bad Debt*, show the array of influences and range of musical tastes of the band.

Although Ann played and sang professionally throughout her adult life, it was just over eight years ago that she and Gaye quit their jobs and decided on a music career full-time. After pooling their money and recording a demo tape (they had been gigging around Fredricksburg, Virginia for a while, and had amassed quite a local following), they forwarded a copy of the tape to Alligator president Bruce Iglauer. Iglauer was impressed by the original songs, by the musicianship of the group, and most of all by the personality that came through the tape. "I just kept coming back to the tape again and again," said Iglauer. "Finally, I figured if I enjoyed it so much, other people would too.

But I never expected what actually happened."

Their debut Alligator album, 1990's *Saffire—The Uppity Blues Women* (AL 4780), became one of the label's best-selling releases. Gaye Adegbalola won a W.C. Handy Award (the Grammy of the blues community) for Song of the Year for her raucous *Middle Aged Blues Boogie* featuring the often-quoted lines: "an old woman don't tell/and an old woman don't yell/an old women don't swell/and she's grateful as hell/I need a young, young man to drive away my middle age blues."

The group quickly went from performing in small, local clubs to performing festivals and concert halls all over the world. They have shared stages with their heroes Koko Taylor,

B.B. King, Ray Charles and Willie Dixon, who said of the band, "They knock me out!" National media outlets like *Entertainment Tonight*, CNN's *Showbiz Today*, and National Public Radio's *Weekend Edition* ran feature stories on the band. Articles and record reviews appeared in *People*, *Down Beat*, *CD Review* and in dozens of major daily, weekly and monthly publications. Saffire—The Uppity Blues Women had definitely arrived.

 Their follow-up album, 1991's *Hot Flash* (CD 4796), featured another collection of traditional sounding contemporary blues. *Down Beat* called the album "a butt-kicking, foot-stomping follow-up...one of the best blues albums of the year." Constant touring and increased radio play earned the group new fans everywhere they went. "Even people who don't like the blues can't resist them," hailed the *Washington Post*.

1992's *Broadcasting* (AL 4811) featured guest players Larry Gray, Tony Zamagni, Steve Freund and Andra Faye McIntosh rounding out the

 sound on the band's strongest collection of original material and classic covers yet. Their subsequent tour brought McIntosh into the band full-time, and with the additional instrumentation, the group jelled into its current and most powerful incarnation. According to the *Los Angeles Weekly*, "Saffire sails along on a rockin', rollin', roadhouse-style path. Their sweetly raunchy combination of cover chestnuts and outspoken originals turn double-entendre lyrics on their head."

Old, New, Borrowed & Blue (AL 4826), released in 1994, was the group's first album to

 feature McIntosh as a full-fledged member. A tribute to their influences, the album mixes classic blues songs with originals inspired by their musical heroes and heroines. Saffire's acoustic music comes from a long history of audacious, humorous, honest songs. According to Gaye, Ann, and Andra, "We embrace the old...we celebrate the new....We've begged, stolen and borrowed a variety of songs, rhythms, textures, licks and tricks." Media attention continued to grow. National Public Radio's *Fresh Air* featured the band, as did *Ms.* magazine in a full page article.

 Now, with *Cleaning House*, Saffire—The Uppity Blues Women continue where their influences left off. With their take-no-mess originals and their fierce, independent attitude, Ann, Gaye and Andra Faye continue to mine blues territory rich in music, deep in history, and full of emotion. In recognition of their talents, the group received a 1995 W.C. Handy Award nomination from the Blues Foundation. *The Chicago Tribune*, in describing one of their concerts said, "These three middle-aged women look more like fugitives from a Tupperware party than a typical blues band. But appearances can be deceiving, as these musicians demonstrated by tearing up the stage with their sassy, funny attitude and their high-powered, take-no-prisoners approach." With *Cleaning House*, one thing is clear: Saffire—The Uppity Blues Women are in a class by themselves. And the story of their success is still being written.

 ALLIGATOR RECORDS & ARTIST MGMT.
P.O. Box 60234 · Chicago, IL 60660
312-973-7736   312-973-2088 (ax)
http\\:www.alligator.com

The opening paragraph of Saffire's bio focuses on the band's "hook"—the uniqueness of their sound. The remainder of the bio blends information about the band's formation with comments on each of their albums.

the-trees" syndrome after they're read a draft several times, when they look straight at an error and it appears correct.

The Song-by-Song Capsule List (Optional)

If the project involves a CD-length work, you may elect to include a track-by-track description at the end of the bio. This is definitely optional, but it may prove useful, especially if a number of songs on the album contain lyrics with real significance. If so, you'll find that many writers and TV/radio people will want to use this information. Keep the song descriptions very short and to the point—about two to three sentences. Use phrases like "concerns child abuse," "describes two people who meet on a plane," "is set in the Caribbean."

THE FINISHED PRODUCT

The final bio will be something the writer, and any co-producers, can be proud of. In a national campaign, thousands of people in decision-making capacities will read it. And you'll be astounded at how heavily they depend on the artist's bio. It's one of the most underrated devices in the business of pop music.

7

THE FACT
SHEET

A short, simple document, the fact sheet has become very important in recent years. It serves as a companion to the artist's bio, but it has fewer and more specific uses.

Back in the early 1980s corporate publicists (who, along with their sports counterparts, currently have the most efficient reputation in the world of PR) started including "data" or fact sheets in their press kits. The practice caught on quickly because these little items proved very useful. Today, the fact sheet is an expected component of just about any press kit, and it lends itself nicely to the aims of the music publicity hunter.

The fact sheet, a kind of abstract of the bio, is a key document in two situations where time is usually critical: electronic media coverage and the closing stage of a print article preparation. In each case the fact sheet lists the dozen or so most germaine facts about the client. Where the bio gives an accurate wrapup of the client in a short read, the fact sheet gives a good thumbnail glimpse of the client in seconds.

IMPORTANCE ON RADIO AND TV

In cases of TV and radio talk shows, the producer and host will usually have read the bio in preparation for the client's appearance. However, since any electronic host deals with several guests on a daily or weekly basis, it's impossible for that person to remember all pertinent details—especially once the on-air light is lit. And in a time-sensitive situation it's awkward for the host or producer to look over a bio—even one that's heavily marked or underscored. So it becomes very important for both producer and host to have the fact sheet at their disposal during the client's appearance. The item-by-item entries on the fact sheet give the host bits of information, so he or she can keep the questions coming at a rapid pace.

It's also common for talk-show guests to cancel on short notice and for others to be booked on equally short notice. This cuts down the producer's and host's already short preparation time. In these instances the fact sheet becomes the most important piece in the client's entire exposure schematic.

Regardless of the confusion, tempers, and chaos that may be going on behind the scenes, the TV or radio talk-show host must appear calm and informed. The properly prepared fact sheet allows a host—who's never heard of the band—to glance over the material seconds before the on-air cue and begin with, "Welcome. So you are from Chicago. Tell us about how you got together. . . ."

IMPORTANCE IN PRINT MEDIA

The fact sheet is an extremely handy, and even critical, item for various types of people working under the print-media umbrella. Depending on personal approach and deadline limitations, there are numerous ways that a newspaper article, album review, or magazine feature story may be prepared.

Some writers carefully compose their pieces step by step and come out with virtually flawless copy. Other equally talented writers prepare a rough draft at something approaching the speed of light, ending up with a jumble of sentence fragments that read like a cartoon character who's had too much to drink.

Regardless of the preparer's personal style, each of these drafts has to be fact-checked before the article goes to press. In many instances writers or reporters do this themselves before submitting the story. In other cases—such as with a big metro daily newspaper or a national magazine—a separate person will handle the fact-checking. Numerous larger magazines have full-time staffers who do this exclusively.

Checking facts is an important phase in the birth of any article, and in this function the fact sheet is without equal. The writer or editor can set it up on his or her desk or copy holder (a clipboard device that sits beside the computer) and quickly check off 50 to 85 percent of the hard facts in the story.

FACT SHEET FORMAT

The fact sheet makeup is simple and blunt. Compared to the bio, it's like a wide-angle view or a quick camera scan. On one page, it spits out the most pertinent data about the client.

The opposite page shows an example, set up for a fictitious experimental rock band. Fact sheets for technical, studio, or corporate clients can easily be tailored along similar lines.

FACT SHEET TIPS

Include small "fact tidbits" that make good springboards for questions. These are very useful for electronic- and print-media people. They make for better interviews, especially when the interviewer knows little about the client.

Be certain to keep the fact sheet to one page. Make the entries concise and clear. Short phrases and sentence fragments are okay in this format.

Always include a contact person and phone number at the bottom, for safety's sake. The fact sheet may get separated from other press kit materials in someone's office; when the fact sheet is being used, the need to get more information may arise and it may be necessary to contact the publicist on short notice.

FACT SHEET
HEAT SEEKERS

Hometown: Orlando, FL

Musical Idiom: Experimental rock/"electronic theater"

Latest CD: Space Pixel's Dream Vacation

Latest Single: "Love Is a Printed Circuit"

Members/Instruments: xxx, keyboards, MIDI, vocals
xxx, guitars, vocals
xxx, basses, vocals
xxx, percussion, various instruments, vocals

Record Label: Ozone Records, Los Angeles

Management Firm: Boxoffice, Inc., San Francisco

Points of Note: Much of the Heat Seekers' music centers on outer space and parody/satire themes; xxx and xxx made their own electronic instruments; their stage equipment was designed by xxx, computer genius and recluse.

Additional Data: Current tour opened in New York on [date]; tour ends in [place]; perform at an unusual venue on [date]; a percentage of proceeds from the New York show will go to xxx technical and scientific scholarship fund.

Contact: Joan Smith 415/111-0000
E-mail: Heat@xxx.com
Web: heat/s@www.com

8

PRESS CLIPS

Known in the industry as "clips," "tearsheets," or "reprints," press clips are photocopied samples of articles that have previously appeared on the client. Clips are employed to give a slightly more in-depth view of the client than that supplied in the artist's bio. On a more subliminal note, they show that other media are paying attention to the act. The latter point can be important to breaking or emerging groups (or other lesser-known clients): it helps reinforce the message "There's something important going on here."

SELECTING CLIPS

The first key to choosing clips is to sift through them carefully. When possible, pick out the best-written and most informative articles about the client. Make a list, in descending order of importance, from the biggest and most credible publications downward.

There's a wide range of possibly useful items that may have already appeared in publications. These include feature stories, concert previews, album reviews, artist interviews, trade-magazine articles (including brief "capsules"), and columns from newspapers and magazines.

Pick the pieces that are the most illuminating and accurate. If a story contains a modest amount of criticism, that's okay. However, avoid the real "slags" or totally negative stories, except in certain special cases.

Good Press/Bad Press

"I don't care what you write," the cliché goes, "just be sure to spell my name right." The idea—dating at least as far back as vaudeville—that *any* press coverage is worthwhile brings up one of the questions most often asked by young band members and others wanting to learn more about PR: Is all press coverage—even the negative—necessarily good for a client?

The answer is that this often depends on the act you're publicizing. As a general rule, negative press is not desirable for a musical client and should be avoided, when possible.

The main exception lies in the "outrageous" corner of the music industry. An outspoken and/or unruly "bad-boy" (or "bad-girl") artist or rock band can actually benefit from negative items in the press. Fans of these artists love to identify with the antics of the stars (or pretend to be shocked by them). So even if the act has been nailed by the press, the fans will cling to the act more devotedly than ever. In publicizing artists that thrive on bad press, some agencies have made mileage, in a campy sort of way, out of deliberately including shock headlines and the most vitriolic, sarcastic copy that they've been able to scrape together.

A word of caution should be inserted here, though. A negative, anarchistic, or bad-guy image can be difficult or impossible to shake off in later years. The artist who has reveled in such an image in one age bracket may one day find himself a little older and wanting to be taken seriously. That old image often proves to be doggedly persistent.

Press Clip Tips

When you're in the narrowing-down stage of potential clips, overlook nothing. And that includes college and high-school newspapers and literary publications. Look for articles and interviews that expand on topics not really covered in the bio—tangential, class-B stories that are still interesting.

A day-to-day rule is that the newer the artist or other client, the better use you'll have for clips. The more established the act is, then the less useful the clips will be (unless there's an outstanding, beautifully written piece in a top publication like *Musician* or *Rolling Stone*).

The first rule in the final decision stage is *don't overstuff*. This has been a problem in the past when eager publicity hounds, proud of their activity files, put a dozen or more clips in a press kit. Beware—this amount of material tends to make just about any journalist's eyes glaze over.

The number of clips included in a press kit should be tailored to the individual client, but a very loose rule would be: an emerging act, one to four clips; an act with two or more CDs, one to three clips; a star act or client, two of the best and most current pieces. This rule varies, depending on the client's situation and the overall quality of the clips. Some acts—esoteric ones, for example—tend to generate better overall reading than others.

For a superstar client, omit the clips entirely. Media people will have heard it all before. And by that point they'll have their own list of questions already in mind.

LAYOUT

In a business where few things are easy, here's an area that's a relative breeze. Laying out the "masters" for your clips is quite simple. Use a razor knife to cut

Read All About It!

February 24, 1994

★ ★ ★ ★

FORCE OF NATURE
Koko Taylor
Alligator

From the opening sting of Criss Johnson's guitar through the open-hearted, deep-soul balladry of "Nothing Takes The Place of You," *Force of Nature* forces the listener to hear Koko Taylor with fresh ears. Though Taylor has long claimed the title of Queen of the Blues, such coronation seemed more a matter of lack of competition than depth of artistry, a reflection of raw vocal power rather than stylistic range -- her blustery swagger limited to variation on the theme of "Wang Dang Doodle."

Force of Nature, however, finds Taylor attaining a royal level of accomplishment, one worthy of Muddy Waters, Bobby "Blue" Bland or any of the various Kings. While it might seem that the last thing the world needs is another version of "Born Under a Bad Sign," the tribute to Albert King finds Taylor and guitarist Buddy Guy tearing into the tune as if it were a sizzling T-bone, with Taylor spurring Guy into a more spontaneously charged performance than often marks his own recordings. Even more familiar and more inspired is "Hound Dog," sparked by a rhythmic arrangement that lets Taylor make the song her own.

The range of the album's material shows Taylor's mastery over several shades of blue, with her phrasing on "Fish in Dirty Water" matching the full-bodied horn arrangement of Gene "Daddy G" Barge in both sophistication and command of dynamics. She swings with sprightly assurance on "If I Can't Be First" and so thoroughly transforms "Bad Case of Loving You" (the Moon Martin-Robert Palmer hit) that it takes a verse or so to recognize the song in its grittier groove.

For all of the album's career-capping, audience-broadening ambition, the music never suffers from overcalculation or crossover contrivance. There's a charge of immediacy throughout that's more common to the midnight bandstand than the recording studio, particularly in the interplay of co-producer Johnson (one of Chicago's finest young blues guitarists, though he more often plays in gospel context) and keyboardist Jeremiah Africa. As for Taylor, there's nothing pretty in her gravel-gargling tone, but she sings with a conviction that shakes life into even the hoariest blues cliches and makes them ring contemporary and true. -- DON MCLEESE

January 31, 1994
Vol. 41, No. 4

FORCE OF NATURE
Koko Taylor

Koko Taylor doesn't take any guff from anyone, including Father Time. Instead of being coy about her age, the reigning Queen of Chicago Blues proudly announces it here in "63 Year Old Woman," an exuberant tune that includes the promise, "If you ride my pony, I'll roll you from song to song."

Saddle up, folks, because this is a woman who's true to her word. More than four decades after the late Willie Dixon rescued her from her day job as a cleaning woman and put her onto a Chess Records roister that included Muddy Waters and Howlin' Wolf, Taylor is still belting out blues in a gravel voice with ferocious intensity. Former Chess mate Buddy Guy joins Taylor's working band here to help pay tribute to late guitarist Albert King on a searing version of "Born Under a Bad Sign." And harp man Carey Bell wails away as Taylor gives fair warning in "Mother Nature" to any woman who fools around where she shouldn't. "I'm lookin' for my man," she sings. "I'm serious as a heart attack/Now one of you women stole him/And I mean to get him back."

The best blues have an earthy grit, and Taylor is not one to smooth out any edges. The result here is foot-stomping music that's rough, raw and wonderfully upbeat from a veteran, no-frills vocalist who doesn't do it any other way. "Don't mess with Mother Nature," Taylor warns. "You know you'll be sorry if you do." (Alligator)
■ DAVID GROGAN

In Koko Taylor's press kit, the press clips are two album reviews presented on a split page and provided as part of a packet of information concerning the blues singer.

JUNIOR BROWN

CURB

The New York Times

THE ARTS
SATURDAY, JANUARY 29, 1994

Review/**Pop**

Cowboy Hat, Jacket and Tie

By JON PARELES

Junior Brown is a country throw-back, an old-fashioned honky-tonker, with a twist. The 41-year-old songwriter has been a local phenomenon in Austin for some time, but his first nationally distributed album, "Guit With It" (Curb), was released last year. Mr. Brown sings about a 'hillbilly hula girl' and about long nights at roadhouses; in one song, he's a singing janitor, while in another he runs into an old flame and reminds her, "You're wanted by the police and my wife thinks you're dead." His voice is a droll, unflappable baritone steeped in Ernest Tubb, Ray Price and Lefty Frizzell. He can yodel, too.

He plays an instrument never seen in country music (or elsewhere) before: the guit-steel, a doublenecked contraption that grafts together a six-stringed guitar and a steel guitar. With it, Mr. Brown answers his own vocal lines or sets forth wryly virtuosic solos. Most country bands have full-time lead guitarists and steel players; Mr. Brown does three jobs at once, four counting the songwriting.

At Tramps, on Wednesday night, his band used only bass fiddle, snare drum (played with brushes) and acoustic guitar (played by Tanya Rae Brown, his wife); the music used unhurried oom-pah rhythms that have eased generations across beer-soaked dance floors. Mr. Brown wore a jacket and tie with his cowboy hat; he's a traditionalist, not a new traditionalist, skipping the sentimental nostalgia of performers like Randy Travis. And he has the genial poise of his models, never milking a song or exaggerating his efforts.

He simply let his fingers do the flying. He applies all the devices of country, blues and bluegrass guitarists: speedy bluegrass picking, plain-spoken melodies, chickensquawk repeated notes, melting steel-guitar chords, skidding fast runs and the deep twang of a bottom string being retuned downward. As if Mr. Brown could split his personality, the smooth tone of the steel guitar contested the wiry attack of the six-string; he didn't run out of ideas.

He doesn't pretend to be old-fashioned; one ballad denounced people who believe the homeless "choose to live that way," and Mr. Brown played a surf-rock medley, including "Walk Don't Run" and "Secret Agent Man." Clearly, he

Junior Brown

Jack Vartoogian

doesn't play honky-tonk country out of insularity, but because he loves it. "I live in the past,' he sang, in a forlorn love song. "But for me, it's a way to survive."

1301 16TH AVENUE SOUTH, NASHVILLE,TN 37212 PH 615-320-1914 FAX 615-320-1731 ★ 250 WEST 57TH STREET, SUITE 2316, NEW YORK, NY 10107 PH 212-977-8111 FAX 212-977-8117

A basic page layout for a one-article press clip—in this instance, a concert review of country artist Junior Brown—includes the name of the publication from which the clip originated at the top, followed by the column or section from which it was extracted.

out the applicable pages and use 8½ x 11-inch copy paper for the background. If the article is laid out in odd-sized blocks and columns, cut each of them into squares, columns, and rectangles that will fit your background paper. Also cut out the publication name and dateline in small rectangles, leaving a small amount of white space around each piece.

Then, using a ruler or T-square, center and square the article on the background, beginning with publication banner and dateline. Use a small amount of paper cement to hold the pieces in place.

Some articles may "spill over" in single columns from page to page in the original. You can cut these into workable columns and line them up on your background paper side by side to save space. The important point is that the finished master look neat, with print columns parallel to the edges of the paper.

Then you're ready for photocopying. Most copy machines today will allow you to reduce and enlarge the original, but be careful here. Don't shrink the story so much that it's hard to read. And don't worry about color copies; black-and-white is fine. Shoot for the cleanest, clearest copies you can get, so your clips are easy to read even after they've been faxed, which tends to degrade the image somewhat. Unless you have a great copy machine, don't worry about how the photos in the article are reproduced. The story is the important item in clips.

Mark Pucci, a successful independent publicist and owner of Mark Pucci Media in Atlanta, describes the overall value of press clips as follows:

> I think that articles, especially for a band that has not been out there that long, can really benefit a writer looking for a story idea. If you only send a bio and photos, lots of times the [media] person will figure it is only from the point of view of someone associated with the band, and usually the writer is looking for other sources of input. Tear sheets can be a big help in that area.
>
> Also, PR can leapfrog off of other PR. It is like a chain reaction. Often I have seen PR that has appeared in one medium open up new areas for us.
>
> I've had clients who, for example, had stories in *USA Today*. The people at a network TV late-night talk show saw the story and decided they wanted the client as a guest.
>
> The media people you are dealing with are very conscious of what is going on with their competitors and the other mediums. Editors are very hip to what is hot and what is not. An article in *Playboy, People,* or *USA Today* can be very helpful.
>
> I am a very big believer in tear sheets. I do think you should get a good representation of clippings. I like to have a really nice interview, record reviews, and live reviews if possible. That shows that the band is well-rounded, not just one-dimensional. But don't overload the press kit. Include five clippings at most with the bio and photos. I have seen press kits that had fifteen to twenty-five tear sheets. I think that is redundant and it has a negative effect.

9

PHOTOS

The photo is probably the most striking part of the music publicity press kit, and often the most effective. But the photographic world can be a bewildering and expensive labyrinth for the hard-pressed publicist. It needn't be. The rules are fairly simple and a few guidelines will go a long way toward getting you a workable, nicely done product. There are numerous talented photographers in just about any geographic area who can help you add a vital dimension to the professional press kit.

The following is an introduction to entertainment photography from a publicity perspective. It will help you get the best work for your client and avoid various costly mistakes.

THE VISUAL ASPECT OF PUBLICITY

In an era marked by computer graphics and high-grade videotape, and with digital video now commonplace, the tried-and-true form of still photography is holding its own as an artistic medium. On the practical side, professionally shot and well-chosen photos of your act can add immense amounts of exposure mileage to your promotion plan.

Print editors and electronic media producers are in constant need of high-quality photographs for use in their shows and publications. They know that illustrations hold an important part of reader and viewer appeal. At the same time, photos have a significant psychological impact on the music consumer. The visual image of your act, reproduced in a newspaper or magazine article or shown on TV, drives home a powerful mental imprint to the reader. Fans or potential fans who see the image will remember the act and be more prone to making a buying decision—much more so than those who have not been able to visualize the artist. In a business that hinges on image, photography represents "image" in its most immediate form. A cliché for sure, but in music publicity this concept is also an axiom: "A picture is worth a thousand words."

FINDING A PHOTOGRAPHER

Locating a person to shoot your modern music act or engineer-producer doesn't have to be a headache. Regardless of your locale, a few phone calls will reveal the top two or three entertainment photographers in your city. The first and most accurate place to start is the local grapevine or word-of-mouth. Ask around and contact entertainment editors, radio station promotion directors, colleagues at other labels or PR firms, and nightclub managers. This technique is also best for locating photographers in distant cities, a common need for publicity people. Your own or a friend's contacts in the local entertainment community should serve as the best starting point. Another good source on a national level is a photographer's representative firm.

Your first choice should be a person with experience in the music business. Most professional photographers tend to specialize—as in product shots, table-top work, or architecture—so hold out for a person accustomed to pop music.

Wherever your location, finding this kind of photographer shouldn't be a problem. One reason is that there's a deep artistic affinity between photographers and musicians: both are involved in highly expressive, personal work. Another reason is that many photographers enjoy musical projects, which tend to be more fun and more artistically rewarding than other types of work. Often you may find that the correct photographer for you is also a musician, or at least a devoted music fan.

When your list is assembled, set up appointments and start looking at portfolios, the visual resume of any good photographer. Most portfolios will include widely differing subjects, compositions, and styles. Zero in on the entertainment stuff—concert shots, CD covers, studio portraits, and shots of parties and other functions.

Talk to the person about his or her experience. Does the person seem to have a feel for your client's music? Does he or she appear enthusiastic about the project? Trust your first impressions about the portfolio and the person, but do your homework. Don't be timid about references and previous clients. Contact a few of them and ask how the sessions went. This initial research is important for just about any music project, from simple group shots (called "group-and-grins") at a release party to a CD cover or a complete photo library.

Also, the person chosen will at times be seen as representing you, your act, and your label or management company in public, at business functions, and to the media. The pro you choose should dress acceptably, have a congenial personality, and be ready to answer just about any photographic question in layman's terms.

PLANNING THE SHOT

Once your photographer is chosen, it's time for the initial planning. At this stage the publicity person can have a big impact on how smoothly the process unfolds.

No matter who the artist is, you and the photographer should start with some kind of basic concept. While undoubtedly bright and talented, the photographer is not a mind-reader and will need some sort of initial creative input. If the project is not large enough to have an art director (many music shots aren't), this is where you, the publicist, might have to step forward.

Right away, get the newest recorded material to the photographer, since he or she will want to preview it and get a feel for the act's music. If at all possible, arrange for the photographer to see a live performance or studio rehearsal. If there is video material on the act, send that also.

Next, arrange a short meeting with the photographer, band spokesperson, manager, yourself, and any other concerned parties. The band will undoubtedly come with a concept of how they want to be shot, and the photographer will probably have worked up some of his or her own ideas. Discuss them all and work as a coalition.

The above illustrates an ideal set of circumstances. If the band's schedule is extremely hectic—as happens when they have a suddenly exploding hit record—there may be no time to meet with all the parties. In this case do the best you can and work with the photographer closely. It may be that the first time they meet the act is at the photo session.

Many music-business "shoots" are very straightforward and don't require an awful lot of planning or setup time. Such situations include headshots of an industry executive or the interior of a studio or management office for use in technical or business publications. Music publicity people are often called on to handle these modest projects. Your planning would consist of arranging the day and time and making sure everyone shows up.

PUBLICITY SHOTS

These critically important photos, included in every press kit, are more complex and require more attention on your part. They face stiff competition from other PR camps, so to be successful they have to be artistic, well-composed, and striking in appearance. In addition, they should capture the artist's personality and should "say" something about the act, whether the shots are posed or live. The prints shouldn't be too dark for good newspaper reproduction, and they should be in perfect focus. Properly conceived, shot, and reproduced, these photos may appear in hundreds of newspapers and dozens of magazines around the country, or even around the world.

If the photos are for a superband or a major label, you—as an in-house publicist—may not be included in the process. Instead the label art people or outside consultants may take over. But if the work is for a small management company or independent label, you may be it, buttonholed to take care of the entire project.

In the latter case, first decide on the basic image toward which to work. Is the best way to go with an outdoor scene or a studio shot? Each choice has its distinct advantages, and the ultimate decision will depend on what artistic product

This stark urban environment provides an appropriate setting for bluesman John Hammond.

JOHN HAMMOND

the rosebud agency
P.O. Box 170429
San Francisco, CA 94117
415-386-3456
Fax: 415-386-0599

pointblank

This rural setting projects the desired image for country bluesmen Cephas & Wiggins.

BOOKING:
Traditional Arts
TEL. (206) 367-9044
FAX (206) 364-2390

Cephas & Wiggins

ALLIGATOR RECORDS
P.O. BOX 60234
CHICAGO, IL 60660
TEL. (312) 973-7736
FAX (312) 973-2088

you want. Ideally, a hard-working band with a regional popularity base should have at least one current photo done in each environment. As soon as your client can afford it, photo variety offers increased possibilities for exposure.

Location Shots

For outdoor or other "location" shots the possibilities are virtually endless. Regardless of the band's musical style, the members, manager, and you should have at least a rough idea of an effective shot before going in. Often, you can use locations to help portray the band's identity: the interior of an abandoned prison for a moody, angry rock band; a funky old billboard or storefront for a singer/poet/songwriter; bizarre architecture or outdoor modern art for an avant-garde or experimental band; a sunny beach setting for a freewheeling pop band; huge earthmoving equipment for a hard-rock or heavy metal band. The limits here are up to the band's, the photographer's, the manager's, and your imagination.

Do your best to match the music and the concept of the outdoor shot—the more dramatic and eye-catching, the more it will be used. Do not, however, go for something so arty or weird that the individuals aren't recognizable; this will just defeat your purpose.

Permissions and Releases

Whenever possible, get written permission from property owners for location shots (normally quite easy, but if you run into trouble, go elsewhere). With abandoned buildings, this may not be necessary.

For the legal protection of everyone concerned, be absolutely certain that model release forms are signed by everyone in the shot who's not connected with the act, label, or photographer. Photographers will have blank model release forms on hand. A person not connected with the act who is recognizable in a photo and is not covered by a release can sue for invasion of privacy if the photo appears in either editorial or advertising.

Model releases are extremely important, for example, in street scenes. Any passersby in the shot must be covered with releases or you're wide open for a sure-loss suit. The same is true for people in the background on lakes, in country stores, and other location settings. The forms only take a moment, so you and the photographer must take the time. If a person balks, rearrange the scene or wait until that person is out of the frame.

There is one exception to this law: the right to privacy does not apply to people in photographs of actual news events, such as disasters, robberies, and the like. This, however, almost never affects publicity shots; get the model releases and protect the photographer, yourself, your label or company, the management company, and the act. All concerned parties can be—and have been—sued over this issue. Most, thanks to a seemingly minor act of negligence that would have taken only sixty seconds to avoid, have lost.

Benny Carter

PUBLICITY:

IN-MEDIA PUBLICITY
TEN PARK AVENUE STE 19-S
NYC 10016 • 212-447-0077

RECORD CO.:
MUSICMASTERS
1710 Highway 35
Ocean, NJ 07712
Phone: 908-531-3375
Fax: 908-531-9666

MUSICMASTERS
J A Z Z

Jazz legend Benny Carter's photo emphasizes the urban sophistication of his musical persona.

ONE WORLD

JOHNNY CLEGG & JULUKA

BOB MARLEY

INNA ZHELANNAYA

GIPSY KINGS

Putamayo's four-panel portrait of some of the artists appearing on the label's world music album is an effective way of displaying different performers showcased on a compilation.

TISH HINOJOSA

Contacts:
Alisse Kingsley   Mark Pucci
Warner Bros.   Mark Pucci Media
818-953-3485   404-816-7393

© 1996 Warner Bros. Records/Permission to reproduce limited to editorial uses in newspapers and other regularly published periodicals and television news programming.

A plain, straight-ahead photo of Tejano artist Tish Hinojosa is a standard approach to conveying a folksy image of a performer.

This straightforward photo of blues singer-guitarist Tinsley Ellis does exactly what it's supposed to do: portray a musician whose strong suit is his guitar playing.

BOOKING:
Concerted Efforts
Tel. (617) 969-0810
Fax (617) 969-6761

Tinsley Ellis

ALLIGATOR RECORDS
P.O. BOX 60234
CHICAGO, IL 60660
(312) 973-7736

Studio Shots

Depending on your act, you may decide on the totally controlled environment of a photography studio. Some of the advantages here are that the photographer will have virtually unlimited lighting resources, along with control over backdrops, props, special effects, and other important facets of a good publicity shot. Studio setups can produce beautiful portrait-style photos of your act, and many publications like these because they reproduce well, even in small proportions.

If you hire a studio, there are some basic tenets that should be followed. Shooting time in a studio is expensive, so calculate your budget carefully. Make sure that everyone arrives a little early or at least on time. (These costly hours and minutes can't be wasted.) If you have to cancel a session, call the studio as soon as possible; if you simply blow off the appointment, you'll be billed for all the time that was booked.

Make certain that everyone treats the studio with professional respect. Don't let your band stamp out cigarette butts on the floor, and see that all cans, bottles, and other garbage are put in appropriate trash cans. If the band leaves the studio in a mess, you can bet you'll be billed for cleanup.

Young bandmembers may be nervous in the photo studio at first, so a little clowning around to loosen up is okay. But make sure you keep a watchful eye.

THE PUBLICITY PHOTO LIBRARY

Ideally, over time, you'll build up a library of photo shots. The depth of your publicity picture library will be dictated by budget and the band's career level. (For more information on this topic, see "Photo Library Considerations" on pages 78–79.)

A club band or brand-new act seeking a label deal may be able to afford only one photo. You'll want to work toward one black-and-white, 8 x 10-inch master photo. Choose the location and concept carefully; this photo will have to cover lots of important mileage.

If the act is working on at least a regional basis, it's an excellent idea to have at least one horizontal color slide available. Color printing technology has become very widespread in recent years, and now even newspapers in smaller cities have this capability. So if your band has the opportunity to appear on a local TV show or to be featured in a newspaper's weekend entertainment section—and it can happen even with garage bands—you don't want to be caught without color. Beyond that, it's quite possible for a club-level music act to blow wide open with little advance warning, and only the amateur music PR person is caught without the right photos to back up the exposure.

Bands at the recording and/or national touring level need more than one publicity photo. It's a good idea to have at least one studio shot and one live performance photo on hand. Ideally, these should be available in both black and white and color and—even more desirable—in different compositions for each.

Starting with the first-album stage and beyond, it's ideal idea to have a rich, diverse photo library to call on at a moment's notice. As the act's recording library and popularity progress, the photo file should keep pace or stay ahead. Be ready to back up that cult record or hit single.

At this stage, it's not too early to plan for a variety of live and studio shots, as well as for photos of individual members. Some magazine and newspaper entertainment editors may want to run a mix of photos with a story. These may include live shots, members at home or play, and studio group shots.

Any platinum or really hot breaking act should have a heavy file of black-and-white and color shots in widely differing compositions and varied locations, from candids in restaurants and unusual settings on tour to charity-related shots. The chief reason to have a fat photo file on a hot band is exclusivity. No editor at a national magazine wants photos that have already run in other publications. Also, the promise of really nice, exclusive photography may clinch that badly wanted story in a major publication. When discussing a feature story in a pivotal publication like *Rolling Stone,* the editors will want to see a battery of photos on the act, some old, some new, to accompany the text. In cases of cover stories, big national publications will probably want to assign their own photographer for fresh, exclusive shots.

CD/ALBUM COVERS

The rules for preparation of publicity photos also apply to more elaborate CD or tape cover shots. If the client is with a major label, or if the cover is going to be a nonphotographic rendering such as a painting, an art director will handle the details and the PR person may have little to do with the project. However, with a small label and/or new act, you may be called upon to help with everything from assisting with makeup to carrying electrical extension cables. The important concept to remember is this: others may duck out the door when there's dirty work to be done, but you had better stay there and pitch in—that's the badge of the publicity professional.

COSTUMES AND MAKEUP

The complexity of costuming may vary widely depending on the act's career level. Publicity photos and CD covers may be extremely elaborate for a platinum-level band, requiring special effects people, costume consultants, and stylists for hair and makeup. Depending on label and budget, the publicist may be called upon to help locate and hire these specialists. If you wind up with this task, start with your photographer's recommendations first. Any experienced photographer will know where to find electricians, prop people, and those who deal in special effects, hair, and makeup.

On a strict budget, you, the band, and the photographer may have to do it all yourselves; this is quite common with new bands and club acts. In some cases, you may have to apply a lot of ingenuity by calling on art students, beauty salon trainees, friends, and acquaintances.

A tight budget is not a hopeless situation. Some really dramatic, effective music shots (and covers) have been done this way. When the specter of low bucks rears its ugly head, keep the project simple. Don't panic and don't be negative; it can be done.

PRESS PARTY PHOTOS

There are numerous photographic opportunities available at press parties, and the music PR person is normally in charge of making the arrangements. These functions may be set up to publicize and celebrate a variety of events: a new CD release, the grand opening of a studio, the installation of a new record-label president, or an artist's donation to a charity, to name just a few.

Regardless of the cause, press parties or business/social functions usually have the same format. Members of the press are invited to come eat, drink, and mingle with the luminaries while getting their stories. There may be live performances or previews of music via CD or videotape. These functions can be loud and hectic for the publicist in charge, so careful planning is to your best advantage. (More press-party tips are discussed opposite in the section "Some Added Pointers.")

Getting lots of usable shots of the party is very important for you, the publicist. These pictures will have in-house uses (as gifts to the visiting dignitaries) and will serve an outgoing function in getting you lots of exposure in the trade and consumer press.

Rule number one is: Take Care of the Photographer. Make sure photographers are properly identified on any guest lists. They can't shoot for you if they're outside, being hassled by security people. If the function is going to be both loud and elaborate (most are), you should arrive early and meet with the photographer, who will need to look the place over and get a feeling for lighting, placement of electrical outlets, and other technical basics.

Your photographer will most likely have no idea who's important and who's not, and here's another area where you'll have to step in: be ready to identify band members, label executives, producers, technicians, and other people who are important to the project. Also, any photographer has only two arms. Be ready with a notepad and pen, and work with him or her to arrange a shot-numbering system. If necessary, identify the people in each picture on the spot, starting left to right. If you know everyone, you can do this later, but if there are lots of out-of-towners, get it right as the shots are taken. Nothing is more useless than a party photo where no one can figure out who's in it.

All party conversation is part small talk, part business, and part socializing. If necessary, pick an opportune moment and interrupt conversation in order to get important shots: your label president talking with a bandleader and arranger; other stars who may have dropped by; important press people talking with your act (a great gift and always appreciated); advertising and retail people mingling with the act; and impromptu scenes of various kinds (such as your keyboard player, the producer, and label president hamming it up at the piano).

Engineers, band members, label execs, and journalists rarely care about image at these functions. You're it. So be ready if the photographer needs assistance in any way. That could mean being ready to hold a photo-flash bounce card in extremely dark situations, and without being terribly obtrusive. A good photographer can cover a press party effectively in a short time, so while he or she is working, stay close. You'll get better shots that are more usable and, in effect, yield more for your money.

If the situation is really hectic and you have several tasks to handle at the same time, assign someone you can depend on to help the photographer. Where there's a lot of tension, such as time constraints on photos or a giant album-release party, the photographer may want to bring along his or her own assistant.

Some Added Pointers

Make certain there's no alcohol or tobacco evident in your band's publicity photos, or many newspapers and magazines won't touch them.

Tours sponsored by beer and wine companies are big business in pop music now, so live concert photos and backstage shots call for special attention. Showing banners, placards, and other promotional items is okay, but have your photographer watch out for empty beer cans, overflowing ashtrays, and the like. Photographs at press parties, which will normally wind up in the trade press, are somewhat less touchy. But even here you should aim for group shots ("group-and-grins"), with no one holding drinks and cigarettes. In a hectic party situation, this is not always possible, but try.

Photo Choices

Keep the end result of all this hard work in mind at all times. You want photos that are useful for publication, because they promote your act in a powerful, immediate way. Make every effort to photograph, and then choose, images that are interesting, catchy, and professionally composed. Unless they fit your band's persona, avoid photos that are so outrageous they may be deemed offensive by editors. Even if your client is a violent, flamboyant heavy metal band it's possible—with a little coaxing—to get photos that are interesting and still suitable for everyone from *Musician* to *People*.

Studying publications that run entertainment photos will help you get a feel for what's currently being used. Professional publicists regularly flip through new copies of everything from *Black Music* to *Vogue* to stay tuned in with photographic styles.

Proof Sheets You'll first see the black-and-white photo results in the form of "proof sheets": 8 x 10-inch sheets that hold all the frames in their actual film size, whether 35mm, 2 1/4-inch, 4 x 5-inch, and so on. These are quick-prints that allow you to choose the final shots for for careful printing. Each frame is numbered to help in the selection process. Because 35mm frames are so small, you'll usually have to use a photographer's magnification loupe ("loopie") when examining them. A good magnifying glass may also come in handy when you look at larger photo formats such as 2 1/4-inch. Once the choices are made, you'll order final prints from these proofs.

Color   A more expensive medium, color photography will come back to your office as 35mm color slides. Handle these with extra care because the slides are one-of-a-kind originals, and if lost or smudged with fingerprints, they're gone forever. This is very different from black-and-white photos, where the photographer normally keeps the film and can make you more master prints if needed.

Each of the color slides will be numbered for the selection process. Very often the photographer will send you only his or her final choices of the best color slides. Among these, there will usually be numerous shots of each different pose or image, so to see the subtle differences you will have to use a slide viewer and/or slide projector. Going through dozens of color slides is a time-consuming process, but take care with it. Keep a running count of the slide numbers on a legal pad as you narrow down the choices.

The Photographer's Input   It's always a good idea to trust your photographer's opinion when choosing the final frames, whether color or black and white. The numerous photo choices, all spread out in front of you, can be very confusing in their similarity. The person who took the shots will have a very good sense of which ones work and which don't. In general, you should ask the photographer to indicate his or her choices with a grease-pencil on the proof sheets, or provide a list of his or her preferred slide numbers.

Usually the photographer is also the best person to check for frames where something's wrong, even though it may not be immediately apparent. Some things to watch out for are people caught in the middle of an eyeblink, or who look tired, or who have a weird expression. Other problems include shots that are too dark, too crowded, or where something's amiss, like a rumpled shirt collar or smeared makeup. Sometimes these glitches may not be apparent until the shot is blown up to full size. When choosing an important publicity photo, you'd be wise to order several test prints of the final choices. Then you and the photographer can study them and, if necessary, think about them for a day or so.

RATES AND CONTRACTS

The business of photography has, in the past, been a source of confusion for many music publicists. In the contemporary entertainment industry this kind of ignorance is simply not acceptable, and the rules aren't that complicated.

Like most other artists, professional photographers work under contract. Any pro shooter will have a day rate and an hourly rate, usually with a two- to three-hour minimum. Rates vary widely, depending on the city and the person's track record. All photographic rates should of course be agreed upon up front and put in writing. Costs will include additional expenses such as travel, lab fees, film, and processing.

One point that's not really advertised: it is possible to catch a good photographer in a slack period and persuade him or her to shoot a publicity photo, for example, for less than the normal day rate. This is made easier if the shooter likes the band.

Who Keeps the Film?

The question of film ownership has been a major bone of contention between photographers and band managers. Here's the rule: under normal circumstances the photographer keeps the film, unless otherwise negotiated. The photographer will deliver one master print per ordered frame, unless more prints are specified per frame.

Photo Uses

There's an important concept that has been badly misunderstood by record labels and managers: any photographer's work is covered by the same copyright laws that protect musical works. In practice, this means that the photographer retains all rights to his or her photographs except for the rights that you specifically purchase.

When you pay normal photo rates, you are actually leasing the photographic work for specific uses, and you are not free to do anything with the photo that you wish. Publicity shots are a good example: if you pay a publicity-photo rate, then that's all they can be used for. If the company later decides to use the same print for a billboard, CD cover, or as part of advertising campaign, then additional fees are due the photographer.

This arrangement makes the best business sense for everyone concerned, since no one can really determine what the actual useful life of a photograph will be. So by retaining most of the rights to their photos, photographers are merely protecting themselves up front and retaining financial control over the future of their work.

It's quite possible to purchase all rights to a given piece of film, but then the applied rates are going to be much more expensive. This is justifiable on the part of the photographer, who's giving up all rights to his or her artistic work, forever.

In the world of music PR it's usually inadvisable to buy all rights to black-and-white film. It's too expensive and the odds are slim that you'll reuse any of the prints. There are just too many variables in pop music: band members and labels change, hair and clothing styles go out of date, and so on. If the need does arise, order more prints from the photographer.

Color slides, on the other hand, are going to be more expensive because you're getting the original—a unique piece of film. Again, handle those tiny artworks very carefully.

DUPLICATION: THE FINAL PRODUCT

Once the originals of your photo order have been delivered, it's time to arrange for mass duplication of both black-and-white and color images. There are a few exceptions: if you only need a few prints of a press-party shot, you may be able to get the photographer to make the few duplicate prints at a reasonable rate. But if you need more than about a half-dozen prints, it will most likely be cheaper to send out the master print.

For black and white, locate a mass-duplication house (any larger city has one) and send the master print there. A mass-photo house can also work up logos on the prints, with the band's name, PR agency, label, and other information.

A specialty color lab is the best place to get dupes of color slides. Even though it's more expensive, order "architectural quality" for your slides—they're almost indistinguishable from the originals and they'll look better in publication.

Under *no* circumstances should you send an original slide away to a magazine, TV station, or newspaper. There's entirely too much danger that it will be destroyed or lost in transit. Much to publicists' chagrin, this rule has been often broken, with disastrous and costly results. Send the high-grade dupes and don't even mention that they're copies.

The number of prints and slide dupes you order is going to vary widely, depending on your campaign. The minimum black-and-white mass order is usually 100, and that's okay for a club band. If you're working up a huge national tour, go with 500 to 1,000.

With color dupes, keep the expense close in mind. It's not necessary to have masses of these on hand, but be ready. Your library may contain as few as a half-dozen dupes of each current color shot. Your judgment of the demand is best here. Also, most color labs can turn dupes around on a 24-hour basis.

PHOTO LIBRARY CONSIDERATIONS

Trying to keep your photo library stocked without overordering is a tricky business. You don't want to be caught short-handed, but you don't want to waste your photo budget either. Some excess prints and slides are unavoidable, but don't worry about them; they'll be used down the road one way or another.

Keep in mind the useful life of your photos. The next new CD and tour is going to call for all new shots. On top of that, band members may quit or be fired just as your print order is coming in the door. Poof—the photos are all useless. But you can't be a mind reader.

One way to avoid overordering is to phone in a rush order for more prints only when you need them. Most publications and TV dates have at least a few days lead time during which you can make the order.

But always hold back a few choice prints and dupes in an emergency file. If *USA Today* wants a photo by 10 A.M. the following morning, put your hot little hands on that file. If you can't, they're going to call someone else.

Never destroy photos, no matter how old and silly they may appear. You never know when a book may be done on your band, or a big TV production, or a magazine article about the past decade in music—the possibilities go on and on. So protect those old prints carefully.

SUMMARY

Photographers are an extremely valuable part of your professional team. Logic and business sense dictate that you take care of them. In public, make sure your photographer is treated with respect (some security types love to hassle people with cameras). Make sure that the person gets paid on time. And always keep in mind that the photographer is furnishing you with some of the most useful tools available to the music press agent.

10

OPTIONAL PRESS KIT COMPONENTS

There are many possible variations of the standard press kit format. Depending on the artist you are promoting, or the media target that you are trying to reach, you may consider adding some components to your kit. Tailoring the press kit to its intended target is the sign of a real pro. Most editors, whether electronic or print, will tell you that their desks are riddled daily with poorly done press paks, almost all of which are pitched into "file 13." Amateurish or misdirected press mailings create a lasting negative impression of both publicist and client. Your band has enough hassles without that.

Items that are sometimes added to standard press kits include playlists, rolodex or business cards, and video bios. As the media world becomes more complex and specialized, these differing components will no doubt continue to evolve, and new possibilities will emerge.

THE PLAYLIST

For a club or "copy" band it's very useful to include in the press kit a playlist or a list of song titles. This quickly shows club managers or talent agencies what style of music the act plays and what category the band falls into. A good agent or club manager can tell at a glance if the act is right for his or her club or music hall—if there's enough rock and roll in the band's repertoire, for example, or enough nostalgia tunes.

Be honest and don't try to doctor up the playlist. Print it out on the same size paper as the bio. Also, don't be timid about including the band's original songs.

Several successful club acts have found another nice touch for their press kits: letters of recommendation from selected club managers around their area. This shows professionalism on the management's part (and, between the lines, assures the other club managers that the band will show up on time, play the gig, and not wreck the dressing rooms).

ROLODEX AND BUSINESS CARDS

Recently, music publicity people have begun including rolodex or business cards in press kits. These items include the company logo, telephone, Net/Web data and fax numbers, address, and account representatives' names. This is a really nice touch and implies *"We mean business."*

SMALL PROMOTIONAL ITEMS

Additional promo items come in and out of popularity in music PR faster than the seasons. Over the years, music publicists have sent out everything from heart-shaped mirrors to junk jewelry, logo-imprinted women's panties, calendars, bumper stickers, and all manner of other mostly useless stuff. The main reason for using these tidbits is to grab attention. Unfortunately, their success rate is rather low, given the constant flood of such items in the media market.

The best advice is: don't include this junk in your press kit unless it's truly funny, clever, or useful (such as a pen, penlite, mini-calculator, or calendar). Also, be very careful about items that might be considered offensive, sexist, or otherwise distasteful (no one can remember the band whose PR hack sent out the panties).

VIDEO BIOS

When a writer or editor hasn't seen your band or client live, the video bio—a video cassette that roughly follows the printed bio format—is very useful. It's an item that has really come into prominence in music PR over the last few years. Relatively inexpensive to produce, video bios can feature interview footage with the act coupled with live concert footage, backstage scenes, and auxiliary segments such as short interviews with the producer.

Video bios are particularly useful for new bands, foreign acts who have not toured in your area, and superstar groups who rarely talk to the press. They give the writer or radio/TV producer a full-blown perspective on the act and make the new CD "come alive" with much more impact.

These days, most locales will have at least one video production house that can handle the raw footage, editing, and final production. Compare rates when possible. It's a good idea to have copies available in both VHS and 3/4-inch professional formats.

One word of caution: video bios shouldn't be used as a crutch. It may seem awfully easy to "lazy out" and just pop a cassette in the mail. If it means extra hassle in getting together a long-distance phone interview with a member of your act, you'd still better consider all the options. Don't insult the media person with the video cassette. Journalists can almost always tell when you're going all the way to get them what they need.

Videocassette Formats

At present the dominant vidcassette format is VHS. Newer formats, such as Super-VHS and 8mm are also gaining in popularity, so keep in touch with these developments. Also, industry pundits now say that we'll soon see a whole generation of delivery systems. Be ready. Professional formats are discussed below.

TAILORING A PRESS KIT FOR TV

In the music business, two types of television programming come into play: standard programming and music TV (MTV and similar shows). The following guidelines apply to standard television programming. Music TV is normally handled by other specialists at a record label. If, however, you're a small label or an "indie," you may be the one making the calls. American television's general attitude toward pop music has changed dramatically in recent years. Today there's a long list of network, local, and cable shows that regularly feature rock and pop artists. Every conceivable type of music is being showcased on, among many other programs, Leno, Letterman, Country Music Television, BET (Black Entertainment Television), E! Entertainment, VH-1, CNN's "Showbiz Today," "Live From the House of Blues," and The Nashville Network. The reason is simple: in most cases the producers and the audience are scions of the rock and roll era. It's now possible to gain a great deal of added exposure on commercial TV that would have been unthinkable just a short while ago.

Getting in on this valuable exposure isn't that difficult as long as the publicist is aware of what TV is looking for. In an era of increasing media sophistication, and with technology exploding all around us, it is no longer advisable to send a print-media press kit to TV stations. The competition for TV airtime is incredibly brutal, forcing the publicist to use every tool and piece of knowledge available. And TV producers are quite insistent (and rightfully so) that PR materials be geared to their needs—needs that are often quite different from those of print media people. Sending along a properly tailored press kit accomplishes two important things: it separates you from the herd of amateur publicity seekers, and it can make your client much more interesting to a producer. Keep in mind: *TV is a visual medium.*

The music press kit as tailored for television is not all that different from that for print, but enough so as to require some serious thought.

- First, cut down the number of clips drastically. Choose the best and most recent print article; that's enough.

- Make certain that the black-and-white photo(s) are augmented with a horizontal color slide (a dupe, not an original—you won't get it back).

- If you include video material, make certain to send it in one-inch (professional) format. Also include a VHS videocassette, since most producers and assignment editors have these systems in their private offices.

- It's okay, and even desirable, to include a list of possible questions in the TV press kit.

- In the cover or "pitch" letter (covered in Chapter 11) state clearly why your client will be of interest to viewers. Point out such facts as that your lead singer is also a humorist, or your bass player is a good storyteller. Briefly mention any unusual visual items that apply to the act—think like a camera. (See the Renault/Nugent interview for more information.)

- The fact sheet is very important to TV producers. They often have to decide in just a few moments whether they want to use a particular guest.

When dealing with TV, don't overlook morning, noonday, and afternoon local talk shows and specialty cable shows that may zero in on your act's hobbies, charity contributions, or other out-of-the-ordinary points.

The TV/cable/satellite/video community is a really hot arena now and it shows no signs of abating. With more formats emerging, such as high-density video discs, the idiom will be increasingly important in the foreseeable future. With some preparation you can cash in on it, no matter how weird your band is.

PART 3

MORE TOOLS OF THE TRADE

11

PRESS RELEASES, PSAs, AND PITCH LETTERS

Beyond the press kit, there are numerous other publicity tools geared for specific functions. These help you to tailor your work to given situations—with the ultimate goal of maximizing exposure.

THE PRESS RELEASE

Short and simple, the press release is an extremely handy little device that can generate exposure by the boatload. Although press release items most often wind up in music columns and entertainment calendars, the release can also generate bigger exposure in the form of feature stories, interviews, and radio/TV appearances.

A press release is an announcement to media people about a specific event or a single occurrence. In the music industry, this may take numerous forms: a gig announcement; the upcoming date of a CD release; a change in a tour itinerary; the replacement of a band member; the grand opening of a remodeled studio; a funny anecdote that happened to an act either on the road or while recording. The publicist's cleverness and imagination are about the only limits here.

It is important, however, to make sure that the topic is interesting in some way to the media person to whom you're sending it. Inexperienced publicists often break this rule and try to fabricate releases on items that are too trivial to interest an editor. Remember, editors are only going to use an item that they think will interest their readers, listeners, or viewers.

Format and Style

The press release should be typed or word-processed using double spacing or space and a half, and in almost all cases should be kept to a single page. There is one exception: a longer release might be required for a very technical topic such as the debut of a new recording console. In all cases it's a good idea to use at least one-inch margins—top, bottom, left, and right.

Make certain that your firm's phone number, address, fax number, e-mail/Net/Web data, and your name are all clearly identified on the first page, preferably at the top. Many pros now recommend that this data be shown on each page of a longer release. Press releases longer than one page should be stapled together as a courtesy to the editor. Loose pages that get lost in a frantic media office result in the release being trashed.

All press releases should be written in a clear, simple style; stick to the facts. The best press releases are done in a journalistic "inverted pyramid" format (see diagram), which means that the most important information appears near the top of the page. Always include a brief headline that summarizes the information to follow. Resist the temptation to get cute in the headline; straightforward is best.

The following simple diagram explains how a press release should be organized.

Media Release
Inverted Pyramid Format

Lead: 5 Ws and H (Who, What, When, Where, Why, and How)

Body: Explain lead and details of facts (concisely)

End: Information of least importance should come in last paragraph

As you attack the problem of composing the press release, try to keep the following pointers in mind.

- Use action verbs.

- Make sure the sentences are in the right order.

- Keep conciseness in mind. Some writers find it useful to write a first draft that ignores length, and then edit down the final version.

- Always use standard-size paper (8½ x 11 inches).

- Think of the press release as a "hook." It's bait for music columns, entertainment-gossip shows, and many other outlets. Plus it may very well attract an editor's interest in a longer story.

- Always consider the target. Only amateurs send out "blanket" releases to everybody on the media list. Tailor the press release; it takes time, but do it.

It's a waste of paper to send a country music item to a hard-core metal writer/editor. An exception is when you have an item that's of universal interest, but take care and think it out.

- Before the release goes out, you and a second party should check for data and spelling errors. Media people are turned ice-cold by press releases that contain stupid errors. They show that the publicist really doesn't give a damn about the client.

- Tape cutlines to all accompanying photographs to identify people in the pictures; identification should go from left to right. It's a good idea to include one sentence describing what's going on in the photo. Color slides should always be numbered, with a cutline/i.d. sheet attached to the slide box.

Treat your press releases with care and they'll work amazingly well for your band. Don't "paper" your contacts unnecessarily (every time your lead singer has a hangnail) and you'll get better results when you do send them out. Two effective professional press releases appear on pages 90–91.

Charitable and/or humanitarian deeds are solid gold here.

PUBLIC SERVICE ANNOUNCEMENTS (PSAS)

An often-overlooked device, the public service announcement (PSA) can be valuable for certain music clients. It is most often used for new bands or artists who need all the exposure they can get.

PSAs are brief announcements (similar to press releases) that are sent to non-commercial electronic media such as National Public Radio or the Public Broadcasting System. The PSA can only announce nonprofit events or charity shows. This may sound like a big limitation, but a well-written PSA can add considerable exposure for a hungry client. Also, if your band has its career plan in gear, they should be doing a reasonable amount of freebies for worthwhile causes.

Mechanics

The PSA should be written as traditional electronic copy (for radio or TV). Use short sentences that make direct statements—nothing else. Stick with the five Ws (Who, What, When, Where, Why) and don't clutter the text with adjectives. Include a simple, short headline at the top.

Type or print the copy in double spacing. And as with your other publicity materials, make sure your contact name and phone number are on the top or bottom of the page.

Pronunciation Guides

In the world of TV and radio, pronunciation is critical, so it's helpful to announcers if you write articulation guides in parentheses after any unusual word or name. The key rule here is: don't assume anything. If the name, town, event, or

MYERS MEDIA

FOR IMMEDIATE RELEASE
April 6, 1995

Contacts: Joan Myers
Jon Paris
212-977-8111

JUNIOR BROWN, HIS WIFE (THE LOVELY TANYA RAE) AND HIS BAND

APRIL 26TH & APRIL 27TH

MERCURY LOUNGE
217 EAST HOUSTON
NEW YORK CITY
9:00 PM

Curb recording artist, Junior Brown comes back to New York for special nights at the Mercury Lounge April 26th and 27th.

Junior has been busy touring all year and is getting ready to release an ep entitled **JUNIOR HIGH** in late June. Included on the 5 song ep are tasty versions of "My Wife Thinks Your Dead", "Highway Patrol", "Sugarfoot Rag" and two freshly penned tunes, "Lovely Hula Hands" and "That's Easy For You to Say".

Tickets are limited so first come first serve!!!!
Guit-Steel air guitar playing is encouraged at all show.

1301 16th Ave S. • Nashville, TN 37212 • 615-320-1914 • 615 320-1731
250 West 57th Street, Suite 2316 • New York, NY 10107 • 212-977-8111 • Fax 212-977-8117

This one-page press release announces an impending concert date for country artist Junior Brown. Note that the primary information—the date, place, and time of the performance—is at the center of the release, with information regarding the artist's forthcoming EP presented below.

The Blue Note Presents
For One Night Only • **Monday, July 22, 1996**

*-- a multi-cultural cross of organic world music beats.
Their irresistible stage show and fresh sound have won them fans around the world.*

Who: **Shlomo Deshet**: drums, pots & pans, percussion
Bentzi Gafni: acoustic guitar, bass
Ori Binshtok: jumbush, suz, electric & eight-string guitar, bouzouki
Amir Gwirtzman: bagpipes, pennywhistles, zorna, ney, Thai mouth organ, sop/tenor sax

What: **Will headline at the world-famous Blue Note** in support of their
US debut album ***Mediterranean Crossroads*** (Newance Records-
Musicrama) recorded at Power Station and produced by Steve Boyer
(Eric Clapton, Bob Dylan, Bryan Ferry, Ryuichi Sakamoto, Maggie Estep)

Where: The Blue Note 131 West 3rd Street • 212-475-8592

When: Monday, July 22, 1996 9pm & 11:30pm *sharp*
$7.50 +$5.00 per person table min.• bar only: $5.00

Contact: Jane Blumenfeld • Aliza Rabinoff **In-Media Publicity** 212-447-0077
***The Esta Hotline* • 212-631-4250**

Washington Post:
"Israeli instrumental quartet Esta cooks its musical stew... Their sound simmers with Balkan,
African, Asian & Celtic influences & blends Mediterranean folk with
American style jazz & rock rhythm."

New York Press:
"The four guys in Esta work bagpipes, bouzoukis, zornas, and other idiomatic instruments into a
very hot and smart rock format... Some of the most feverish fun and unusual ethnopop anywhere."

The Village Voice:
" with its chopsapoppin' technique, articulate melodies and blatant disregard for generic
distinctions, suggests Zappa on the Orient Express. ....impressive collective technique...
and world-ranging curiosity."

**Sponsored by the Department of Cultural Affairs in the U.S.
Consulate General of Israel
Esta is Available for Interviews**

In-Media

---

*While announcing an impending concert date, this press release for world music artists musicians
Esta also provides more background information about the group itself—including its members
and their instruments and selected quotes from established newspapers and tabloids.*

hall presents the slightest pronunciation difficulty, spell it phonetically in parentheses. No good air host or newsreader will be offended, and they'll appreciate the touch.

Here's an example, mispronounced on network news: Valdosta (val-dahs-ta).

Length

Keep the copy very short—no more than a long paragraph—and write it in the inverted pyramid format with the most important data at the top. You can include less-important material in a second paragraph, separated by two double spaces, but don't expect everyone to use it. College stations with lots of open air time just might, though.

Timing

Here's the mark of a music publicist with sparks at the fingertips: use a stopwatch and time the copy as it's read aloud. See that the copy falls easily into 15-second or 30-second frames—the time configurations most often used in on-air announcements. Electronics people will really appreciate this (they won't have to edit the copy themselves), and your chances of getting the PSA on-air will be quintupled.

In terms of lead time, try to get your PSA copy to radio and TV stations two weeks before the event. They'll most likely record the material on cassette.

Here's an example of a public service announcement:

June 26, 199x

For more information contact: John Smith 111/231-0000

Emilio Regina to Perform in Benefit at Hi-Ho Club

(30 seconds)

Guitarist Emilio Regina (E-**meel**-yo Ray-**jeen**-ah) will appear in a benefit performance at Atlanta's new Hi-Ho Club on Sunday night, July 16 .... The show, called "Soup for Cats," will benefit homeless felines in the Atlanta area.... Tickets for the performance are $9.00.... For more information call the Hi-Ho Club at 355-0000.... The show is sponsored by Angry Cat Lovers, a new local pro-cat organization. . . . Acoustic guitar master Regina is from the small Caribbean island of Tabbor (Tah-**bore**).... He is famous in his native land for his fiery, passionate style and cat activism.

# # #

THE PITCH LETTER

Known in traditional business correspondence as a "cover letter," the pitch letter is a refined version of this communication tool that has specific uses for the music publicist. This short but vital document is personally written and goes on top of other PR materials, such as a press kit, so it's read first. Like a carnival barker, the pitch letter introduces you and your client to a media person and "pitches" your cause to them. The PR pitch letter is known in the media world as a "We're Great!" But never mind the typical editor's sarcasm; good pitch letters work very well.

Format

A quality pitch letter is written much the same as a standard business letter, and there are numerous acceptable forms. These are easily researched by looking in any typing book, secretary's handbook, or business communication text. A simple "flush-left" format is fine, with return address and date, followed by a space, and then the target address and greeting/salutation, all lined up at the left margin. Fancier letter formats are also okay within reason. Some of these have the date and salutation centered on the page and the rest of the text flush on the left margin.

It is highly desirable to limit the letter to one page. Experienced editors scan the text rapidly and decide in a few moments if they're interested or not. Only in the most complex cases—or when you're dealing with very technical topics—should this rule be broken.

If you're writing a "cold" pitch letter to someone you don't know, stick with a slightly formal greeting, such as "Dear Mr. _____" or "Dear Ms. _____." This is safest. If you know the person to whom you're writing, you can go with a less formal greeting, using the first name.

Keep the tone friendly and positive without being syrupy. As in other publicity communications, you should get to the point quickly. Describe the topic succinctly and then show how your client would be of interest to the particular publication, TV station, or other outlet you're writing to. Whatever you write, don't ramble, even if it takes four rewrites of the draft.

After you've made your pitch, conclude quickly and close with a polite salutation, such as "Sincerely." Include the abbreviation "Enc." below the signature if other material is enclosed.

A lot of exposure may ride on how your pitch letter is perceived, so spend enough time on it and go through all the usual checks: spelling, punctuation, and facts, as well as reading it aloud to spot nonsequiturs (items that do not follow logically), wandering sentences, and unnecessary verbiage.

Following is a sample of a fictional pitch letter in flush-left form.

Your company name or logo
address
phone/fax/e-data numbers

Date

Mr. Jean-Gabriel Costa
RAGS Magazine
161 Barn Street
Centralia, IL 61101

Dear Mr. Costa:

I am writing to you concerning a young performer named Ronnie Lee Hood. I believe that Ronnie may prove of interest to <u>Rags.</u>

Ronnie Lee Hood is a 21-year-old acoustic guitar player and singer whose home is the mean south Atlanta slum of Cabbagetown. Ronnie, who is white, was given a few guitar lessons at age 12 by a black blues player, a local legend named Dexter "Shank" McBride. Ronnie's current musical style is one of the most interesting mixes that I've heard in a long time. His songs combine the classic Piedmont area blues with early show tunes and even some of his Irish/English heritage. His themes are also characteristic: sex, violence, and life on the streets.

If Ronnie Lee's music and lyrics have an authentic, gritty sound, it's for a good reason. He pretty much lives the life he sings about, choosing to stay on his home turf of Cabbagetown. Among his many outside influences are Blind Willie McTell, Leon Redbone, and John Hammond.

I think Ronnie Lee and his story would make an intriguing feature for your readers, who I know are well educated and eclectic.

I am enclosing a press kit for your perusal. It contains the artist's bio, photos by Thomas R. Hill, and Ronnie's debut single, "R Is for Rhythm and B Is for Blues." A quick look, I think, will show why Ronnie Lee has become a headliner at local clubs such as Killin' Floor.

I'd be happy to work with you toward a story on Ronnie Lee. If you don't have a writer in this area, I can recommend several. I look forward to speaking with you soon.

Sincerely,

[Signature]

Enc.

12

REFERENCE TOOLS AND MEDIA GUIDES

Any serious PR person or publicity hunter should have at his or her fingertips a set of basic reference items that ease the day-to-day process of preparing materials and getting them out to the right people. Among these are style and usage books, media directories, and lists of contacts throughout the media world. Let's take a close look at some of these vital desk tools.

REFERENCE BOOKS

Besides being media junkies, most good publicists are also addicted to reference manuals because they're so valuable in the business of communication, whether you're preparing an artist bio or writing a pitch letter. Following is a survey of books that are widely used by professional writers, editors, and PR people. This list only skims the surface of the dozens of outstanding reference works available today. Your personal preference is the bottom line. Today, many reference works are available in print, as software programs, and on CD-ROM.

Any such collection has to be topped by a current volume of *Webster's Dictionary* and one of *Roget's Thesaurus,* the office companions of any literate professional. In addition to *Webster's* there are several on-line computer dictionaries and pop-up thesaurus programs for personal computers. All of the major word-processing programs now come with both dictionary and thesaurus programs built in. If you want added horsepower, "Multilex" (MultiLing International), a PC TSR (transident, stay-ready) or "pop-up" program, has a very large dictionary and thesaurus.

The New York Times Manual of Style and Usage (Times Books) is another reference warhorse. It can help to overcome a raft of verbal stumbling blocks that would otherwise slow you down. ("Money figures: do I spell them out or use a dollar sign and digits?") Academicians can argue until the moon goes down, but if your band is getting ready to hit the circuit, you don't have the time. Trust this book and you'll never be wrong enough to be embarrassed.

Punctuate It Right! (Harper and Row) is a handy little paperback for anyone without a degree in English.

Excellent for both trivia freaks and high-pressure publicists, *The Synonym Finder* (Rodale Press) is an outstanding thesaurus, quite popular with professional writers. Some authors believe it's the fastest and easiest to use of its genre.

The Concise Dictionary of Music (Oxford University Press) is very handy, regardless of the musical idiom in which you're working (it's especially helpful if you're handling a classical or symphonic client).

The above works are just a sampling, but they'll give you an idea of the help books available for professional communicators. Regardless of the type of artist, whether they break out into arias in the hallways or wear spiked mohawks and spit flames without provocation, these volumes will help you produce clear, accurate, and interesting copy.

MEDIA GUIDES

Any record label (other than a brand-new indie) or large management firm will have an established media list, and the same is true for almost all entertainment publicity firms. The media list, whether it's on paper/Rolodex or computer file, holds names, addresses, phone numbers, and editor titles of print and electronic media outlets in the region or across the nation. The established list will also detail names of music writers, independent critics, and nonfiction freelancers who specialize in pop music.

In a perfect world, these priceless resources are your roadmap to the correct people in any city, no matter where the tour or promo junket is going to hit. In reality, media lists need constant attention to keep them updated, because of the ever-changing nature of this kind of data—phone numbers, zip codes, street addresses, and especially the people. There is a constant turnover inside the media, from small weekly newspapers to major TV networks.

The pressure is on you, the publicist, to keep that list up to date to the last semicolon. Few things irritate a music editor or talk-show producer more than receiving a press kit addressed to last month's, or last year's, titleholder. You can imagine their lack of enthusiasm for your act if this happens. Most editors will toss the package in the trash without opening it.

"Last-updated" records should be kept on the actual file, and if the person is not contacted regularly, then call and double-check before your package goes out. It's worth the extra phone expense and will help you avoid wasting paper and postage on a misfired mailing.

"Backup" is a vital term for any publicist. Whether it's on paper or disk, keep backup copies of your updated media list—preferably more than one, and in separate geographic locations. Don't be caught in the middle of a big campaign with a crashed hard drive on your computer (it happens) or files destroyed by mistake (it also happens).

DIRECTORIES

There are a number of good media directories to help in the challenge of keeping a list up to date. Any metro area will have several local media guides, such as those compiled by Women in Communications, Cohn & Wolff Public Relations, and many others. A trip to the library or the nearest quality bookstore is a good starting point.

There are also several very good directories on the national level. A few of these include *Bacon's Publicity Checker, Ayers' Media Guide, Adweek's Media Guides, Standard Rate & Data,* and the *Editor & Publisher Yearbook.* Some of these volumes are quite expensive, so don't overlook the value of your local library if you're on a budget.

By referring to these resources, you can update your office files on Montana or you can put an entire media list together from scratch if you have to. Take advantage of these tools; they'll give you a firm basis for increasing your artist's national exposure. Tip: If you're updating your list, you don't necessarily have to bother the editor in question—the switchboard operator or department receptionist can confirm or give you the new names and other relevant information.

COLLEGE PUBLICATIONS

In terms of keeping a media list current, college newspapers and radio stations represent a key exception to the above rules. These change entertainment editors so rapidly that it's virtually impossible to keep up with them on a national basis. It's perfectly acceptable to address college-bound packages to "Music Editor." But however you address it, don't overlook this extremely valuable exposure genre.

13

TECHNOLOGY IN THE PUBLICITY WORLD

The arena of new technology is changing very, very rapidly. In his excellent book *Being Digital,* computer visionary Nicholas Negroponte sees no end in sight—in fact, the opposite. He predicts that developments in the new technologies will be even more rapid, and more dramatic, in the next decade. With this in mind, the editor and the author have made every effort to give up-to-date, accurate information at press time.

The upshot is that, because this field evolves so swiftly, even by the time this book arrives on shelves, the tools, services, software, and techniques discussed in this chapter may already be out of date or otherwise supplanted. In the author's opinion, it's in the reader's best interest to stay up with the latest in technology and communication. Periodicals, both electronic and print, are a good way to accomplish this. (See the Shaw and Gillen interviews for more information.)

The recent explosion of new technologies, many of them related to information and communication, has dramatically changed the face of the news and entertainment media, and along with it, the approaches used by entertainment publicists. In mid-decade, the enormous upsurge of interest in the Internet and the World Wide Web added another spectacular venue for entertainment PR—the newest plateau in that oft-discussed tier: print, radio, TV, and cable.

Not too many years ago, even the most successful music publicists relied mostly on ballpoint pens, 3 x 5-inch index cards, and rotary-dial phones. For a time in the mid-1980s, there was a stubborn, even romantic, insistence to stay with these, and with the trusty old electric typewriter that had yielded so much exposure for everybody from the Yardbirds to Waylon Jennings and B.B. King.

Whether PR people wanted to admit it or not, the introduction of personal computers (PCs) signaled the end of that era and the dawn of a new one: the realm of truly high-speed communication and mind-warping data-management capabilities.

The continuing (and accelerating) spawn of new technologies by the mid-1990s had radically changed the way publicity people work and even think. There is now an atmosphere of immediacy pervading the media. In an era of intense Internet/Web use, bag phones, national pagers and mini-printers—just to name a few—the publicist must be ready to respond to a request immediately, or the opportunity may be lost. An editor at a daily newspaper such as *USA Today* or a radio host may have only moments to receive information, so demands from media people now have a new sense of split-second urgency.

As we look to the new millennium, in what some are calling the "Post-Information Age," there is simply no question: the person who wants to succeed in this business must be aware of all the new devices and services available—and equip himself or herself with as many of them as possible. With the music industry as it is today (demanding and competitive) and the current level of sophistication in the media, there is no other way you can do an acceptable job for your client.

LEARNING THE TECHNOLOGY

Knowledge, experience, and lack of digital fear are key in today's communications environment. The person who is intimidated by computers, modems, fax machines, and the like will have difficulty from the first day out. But the publicist familiar with all the latest equipment and comfortable with software programs will be ready to handle a variety of situations and get exposure by the truckload.

As this chapter will demonstrate, there is nothing to fear about digital communications and information management. Instead, this technology makes the PR person's life immensely easier and more efficient. More refinements and new product introductions are in the foreseeable future. Each month, it seems, new products, programs, and services are announced that may be useful to the music publicist.

Getting used to the new devices shouldn't be something to dread; rather, it should be an exciting and rewarding experience. Anyone can learn to use computers, fax machines, and the other digital equipment around us. Doing your homework, taking notes, and a good attitude all help. Face it: you will make some mistakes. Everyone else has, and does. So just relax in that knowledge and exercise a little care.

Keep in mind that the newest generation of "Plug-and-Play" PCs—which arrive preformatted and preconfigured—are much, much easier to learn and use than those of just a decade ago.

Here are some tips on learning about personal computers:

• Do some reading. There are several books out, titled along the lines of "Technology for Dummies." Peruse computer magazines as you're shopping. Borrow the manual and study it—any quality computer store shouldn't balk at that if you are considering one of their systems.

- Ask questions and don't be afraid of sounding dumb. That's why the sales-person is there. Talk to hackers who are already "eaten up" with computers. If you can find a user's group, go and hang out.

- Beware of advertising claims. When possible, get a full product demonstration—not a demo program—before you buy. Ask around. Does this product work? Does it have bugs or glitches? Any salesperson at a quality store will gladly install a program and run it for you.

- Take advantage of educational opportunities nearby. Most colleges have courses such as "Introduction to PCs." Find out about word processing first, then beginning data management. Take an Adult Ed course on the Internet or the Web. If you have access to a friend's machine, go through an online tutorial or two. There are also videocassettes available for rent that teach you how to use computers, software, and peripherals.

- Rent a system you like for a weekend and play with it. The cost is minimal in light of your important buying decision.

WHAT TO SPEND

You don't have to spend a small fortune in order to do contemporary music publicity. Many of your decisions will be based on the size of your company, your client roster, and the scope of your operation. If you are a one-person company handling one local rock band, your equipment can, of course, be more modest. You might occasionally find bargains on used equipment from companies who are upgrading their equipment; in the PC world, cost equals power. However, if your firm or label is international and has one or more superstar acts, you'd better be looking at the more recent, faster, and higher-capacity devices.

In the world of consumer-grade electronic equipment today, you get exactly what you pay for, nothing more. There are no bargains unless you are clever enough to discover the occasional loss-leader at big retailers. If you buy the cheapest answering machine or cordless phone, for example, they will perform accordingly for you—cheaply. If you're going to work in a professional arena, you don't need machines that are inordinately noisy or that may quit without warning. All electronic equipment is subject to failure at any time, but the upper-price devices are normally tougher—and smarter.

SERVICE

Before you buy a piece of electronic equipment, find out about warranty conditions and local repair-service/parts availability. Be insistent about the latter. If a machine is going to work hard for you in an office environment, you must have a measure of dependability—and, with computers and software, good factory technical backup. If you decide to purchase a major system, such as a full-blown PC setup, talk to the factory tech people first and see how sharp they are. Tech assistance varies widely from one supplier to another.

Stick with major brands—and that includes PC-clone manufacturers—because they generally have superior backup assistance. If you buy a no-name device at a discounter and it goes up in smoke when you plug it in, you may find yourself in a wire canoe when you try to get it repaired or settle the warranty. It costs a few more bucks to stay with the majors, but it's well worth it—unless it's a throwaway item like a pocket calculator.

If your budget will allow it, by all means arm yourself with professional-quality devices. These are not normally available in retail stores, but the nearest branch office of any big supplier like Sony, Philips, or Panasonic can tell you where their closest pro shop is located. This equipment, from recorders to transcribers to phones, is usually tough as nails, smarter than the prodigy next door, and fast as a blue flame. If you are doing publicity for a dozen bands going in as many directions simultaneously, you need this level of sophistication and dependability.

NOTE: Always use the best quality tape you can find, preferrable professional quality. You want your work to have the cleanest sound possible; also, cheap tapes are prone to breakage.

PERSONAL COMPUTERS

The personal computer has opened up fabulous new vistas for the music publicist. Here's a quick survey of how you can use computers to greatly enhance your office capabilities. Using the latest generation of word processors and/or data-management programs, you can:

- Write, edit, and store documents such as bios, press releases, and pitch letters quickly and easily.

- Edit, revise, update, and tailor your documents efficiently. For example, with a bio, you can keep the original version intact and augment it with more technical information for tech-type publications.

- Correct errors and outdated material in important documents such as bios.

- Store all of your media lists, contact lists, and notes in electronic files—with instant access and cross-access when you need it.

- Customize your mailing list on a project-by-project basis—a very important feature.

- Spell-check drafts that are hastily written, and use an onscreen thesaurus to remedy "guitar, guitar, guitar" repetition problems. Use an onscreen grammar checker to look for passive voice and stylistic errors.

- Produce camera-ready copy (skipping the typesetting process) that is set for photocopying or print-shop.

- Create multiple versions of a complex draft that's giving you trouble, while keeping the original intact. This can help clarify problems in a manuscript.

- Skip the paper process by sending diskette copies of material to other departments, managers, and the like.

- Search for and replace names, phrases, and other terms in a document.

- Make multiple backup copies of key documents for safe storage and/or distribution. This eliminates the nightmare of a one-of-a-kind original paper draft being lost or trashed before it can be copied.

- Do online research and contact work, via modem, which connects you with a galaxy of information—and opportunities. The Internet—a global arena of interconnected computer systems—is now easy to access and navigate. The World Wide Web, the Internet's graphical/commercial arena, holds a mind-boggling array of Web sites—pertaining to every conceivable topic. Hugely popular with music fans, the Web offers graphics, video, and audio, and with the latest programs it is easy to navigate. The News Groups, accessible either through the Web or the Internet, are groups of correspondents interested in a common topic—such as the Big Band era or electronic experimental music.

BUYING AND USING A COMPUTER

When you're shopping for a PC, carefully consider the oceans of advice you're going to get. Purchase the most power that you can reasonably afford. A typical system might be a 486 PC with high-capacity hard drive (600 to 800 meg); floppy drive; CD-ROM; high-speed modem (28,800 or faster); keyboard and mouse; sound card and speaker system; combination printer/fax/copier; VGA color monitor; and, optionally, a scanner.

When you're working on a computer, never leave key files (such as gig sheets) stored on only one source. Hard drives can fail, magnetized objects can destroy data on a diskette, and files can be erased by accident. Diskettes are cheap. Making backup copies of your files only takes a few moments and can save lots of time, for example, in the event of a fixed-disk failure.

Save your files to disk often. Never leave your computer with unsaved material in memory. (Many word processors now have "auto-save" features.)

Always keep floppy disks inside data boxes when they're not in the machine. Follow all diskette-care rules outlined on the disk jackets.

Keep magnetic objects like paper-clip holders away from your computer and data boxes.

Back up your system files (word processors, browsers, and so on) on disks, read/write CD, or tape drive. If using tape, make sure the software is set to 100 percent error correction.

Laptops

Briefcase-size computers are extremely handy for the music publicist who travels often. These machines are now widely seen with large-capacity RAM (working memory), hard drives, high-speed modems, back-lit screens and mini-printers.

Laptop computers are not cheap, but they're now a virtual must for anyone handling a national touring act or with a full client roster. With a laptop as part of your luggage, you can:

- Create, edit, and revise copy on planes, in hotel rooms, and even backstage if necessary (or in other weird places you may find yourself under deadline).

- File or retrieve documents or other data from your office via modem. Also, send and receive E-mail messages and/or check your label's newest Web site postings, monitor contests, chat sessions, and so on.

- Keep up-to-the-minute backstage/press/photo pass lists at a big outdoor show or other complex, demanding event.

- Work in peaceful, out-of-the-way places when you need quiet and the absence of hassle and interruptions in order to finish a real problem assignment.

- Take the work with you on fun/work junkets, in situations when your boss says, "I don't care if you go or not, but have that project finished by Monday morning."

- Stay in touch, via electronic mail, with managers, international department people, and media people who may be in several disparate parts of the world, and still need daily or even hourly input from you. Often talking by phone is not enough; a manager or a promoter in England may want to see a document right away, like on the eve of a big tour opener.

FAX MACHINES

Facsimile (fax) machines are now an absolute must for the publicity seeker. Don't say you can't afford one; you can't afford *not* to have one, period.

Fax machines operate like this: You feed a sheet of paper (generally 8½ x 11 inches or smaller) containing type or an image into the machine and dial the phone number of the distant fax device. The machine scans the material on the paper and transforms that material into electronic data that is sent over phone lines. The distant machine receives that data and then works in reverse, decoding and then printing out a duplicate page—complete with black-and-white or color illustrations, charts, and signatures. The whole process takes only moments, depending on the number of pages, and the documents are legally binding, including signatures on contracts.

The fax/printer/copier combo machines are very useful and efficient. They offer plain-paper fax and are office space-savers.

MODEMS

The telephone modem (short for "modulator/demodulator") connects a PC or laptop to the outside world by a phone line or coaxial cable. Through a modem, computer-file information is encoded into data that can be sent over phone lines or cable. The distant machine gathers in the phone data and then decodes it into computer information that can be stored directly on disk and/or printed out.

Modems can be very useful in both communication and research. Using electronic mail, you can upload messages, press releases, and other documents into electronic mailboxes that are accessible all over the world. You can also transmit information by modem directly into computer mainframes at various media outlets—providing you have prior permission. In addition, the modem is a key component in your Internet and Web connections and to online services such as Compuserve.

VENDORS AND DATABASES

Using a modem, you can log onto any of several multiservice electronic "vendors" like Compuserve. From their main onscreen menu, you can choose a plethora of services, including research on hundreds of databases—some general and some highly specialized.

Using a multiservice vendor such as MCI Mail, you can send and receive E-Mail and also access back issues of various publications as well as scan breaking stories that may concern your client (as fresh as a few hours old for some publications). You can "tag" services to identify and hold mentions nationwide that relate to your client. You can also upload a document from your computer, and have the service send it to a designated fax machine.

Other sophisticated research services, available by modem, include complete encyclopedias. You can search and "narrow-search" major newspapers for topics such as "Robert Cray and 1996"—which will give you only press mentions of that year. It's also possible to global-search across many different publications and back several years—very useful when you need to learn everything in two days about a new client.

ISPs, Browser Programs, and Search Engines

With your modem you can connect to an Internet Service Provider (ISP) such as UUNet. Using a browser program such as Netscape you can go straight to the Web and easily make your way around. Inside Netscape, you might choose a Web "Search Engine" such as Yahoo! or Lycos to look for an almost-infinite variety of topics—like "Whitney Houston tour" or "novelty records the 1950s."

AUDIO

If your system has a sound card and speakers, you can use a program such as Realaudio to get demo material, previews of music videos, new CD releases, and other multimedia data. This is very useful to see what the competition's doing and in your search for ideas.

Your involvement with a Web site may vary. You may need to update bio material, contest information, tour schedules, and promotion schemes. Along with your label's Webmaster, you may help redesign graphics, sound, and text to make your site a true multimedia experience. You'll also likely help plot out future contests.

NOTE: For more information, see the Shaw and Gillen interviews, as well as the recommended reading list at the end of this chapter.

CONTACT MANAGERS: DATABASES AND PIMS

This section was prepared by James T. Bass, co-author of *The Modem Coach* (New Riders Publishing).

Databases and Personal Information Management programs (PIMs) can be extremely important to the entertainment publicist in the never-ending quest for better organization. Data management and manipulation skills are imperative for today's media arena.

Databases

Database programs in general are a real boon when it comes to manipulating data that can be put into patterns: fields, records, and files. The information is divided into repetitious groupings so that within a file many records can be input field-by-field. Then it can be searched, reported on, indexed, sorted, browsed, deleted, appended, or edited. The reports can be just on the screen or can be printed out. Address database programs with accompanying data files are used to print labels for mass mailings, or for on-the-road phone books, complete with notations.

Database programs can be quite beneficial, but it is extremely important to understand the basics of how they work. A separate—although not difficult—language is required to program a database so the information can be placed into it efficiently and extracted in a meaningful way. The three major steps in working with databases are file design, data input, and data retrieval. Information in a database is handled with fields, records, and files:

- Fields are individual pieces of information that can be searched, sorted, and reported on.

- Records are blocks of information made up of one or more fields.

- Files are made up of one or more records.

Databases come in a few different styles:

- A fixed database comes already programmed for specific information and purposes.

- A flat file database must be programmed with all data in one database file.

- A relational database must be programmed and can have several database files sharing data connected by a common field in each.

A fixed database is a specialized program already designed for the convenience of the user. An example of this is a contact management program, which keeps track of when and how contact is made. It can remind the user when future connections need to be made and can keep track of what is said. Of course, the data has to be typed in and kept updated by the user. Another example is an address book and dialer program. This useful device can print labels and reports and can dial numbers from your address lists.

An example of a relational database program is Alpha 5, a Windows-compatible nonprogrammers relational database that is run by menus in an easily understood progression of steps. Alpha 5 enables even a novice computer user to design multiple database files so they interact. With a little work—but without programming skills—you can conquer the world of data by creating reports, lists, labels, and forms.

Personal Information Management Programs (PIMs)

There are several PIMS on the market. One of the most useful is Info Select 3 for Windows from Micro Logic. Info Select was a TSR program (Terminate/Stay/ Resident) in the DOS system, and has now become even more effective as a Windows program. Info Select is a Free Form database and more. A Free Form database does not require particular types of data in predesigned fields; each "record" can be organized differently and have different quantities of information.

As a Windows-compatible program, Info Select 3 is activated and left running in its own window. If you choose, this window can be forced to the top of the Windows desktop at all times. It can also be minimized, or be placed behind the active window. Data can easily be copied from Info Select to the other Windows-compatible programs (such as a word processor, for example).

Info Select 3 can have whole files or blocks of data sent to it or pulled from it. You can organize that data in any way that makes it easy for you to work with the information. For instance, if you are a publicist for several groups, all of which are on tour, you can set up several groupings of information, one for each tour or group (electronic gig sheets).

Each packet of information can contain files of data pertaining to that particular tour. Any time you need to add a sub-window for new information, or add information to an existing sub-window, you just click on it and input the data. This means that you can have a window containing sub-windows, holding phone numbers with names and locations, dates with locations, crew members names, plus lodging and other special data for specific dates, and so on. The beauty of this database power is that you can specialize and customize information in any way you need. If a national magazine, for instance, has a really complicated cover shoot in a distant city, you can easily and quickly stay on top of the minutest details.

Important contacts, unusual media information for particular shows, who's on first, and other details can be put in as needed. The data group can be activated with a simple click. With a only a few clicks of the mouse the specific information wanted is brought forward. It is then looked at or placed, in part or whole, within another file that is being worked on. The specific window is brought forward by searching through the groupings of data. If you want, it can be placed in a current document by "mark," "copy," and "paste." With this digital muscle at your fingertips you can shape and tailor your media lists, for example, to suit even the weirdest event and circumstance.

A PIM can make a day on the phones productive instead of having to look up every individual bit and byte of information separately. There are many PIMs out there. Look around for the features you want and ask salespeople for demonstrations of the actual product before buying.

TELEPHONE OPTIONS

Obviously, the phone is one of the most critical devices for the music publicist. For your desk unit, there are a number of very handy options these days, and you should be aware of all of them. One of the most important is the memory feature that allows you to code in dozens of your frequently dialed numbers. The redial feature is also mandatory; it's maddening when you have to contact a writer in Vancouver and keep getting a busy signal. Even with this feature, your dialing fingers will be sore enough at the end of a long day. Also, the more tired you are, the greater area the chances of hitting a wrong digit—and then you have to start all over.

Three-way conference calling is another inexpensive feature that's widely available today. This is particularly useful for crisis situations, or for resolving mixups with two outside parties who may be in different parts of the country.

Voice mail is 100 percent efficient and very popular in PR these days. If your label or firm doesn't have a full interactive system that provides options—leave a message, talk to the operator, talk to another department, and so on—you can order or design an inexpensive one. Most local phone services now offer voice-mail options.

You can also connect an answering machine to your phone when you're out. If you're out for any length of time, check with it on a regular basis—don't let a bored fellow employee or switchboard temp garble a last-minute crisis call from a major publication or network. Imagine how you'd feel if you had to tell your boss that the story was scrapped because certain facts couldn't be checked.

Any pro PR person should also have voice mail or an answering machine on the home line, as well as a listed phone number. This is imperative because situations of all kinds can crop up at odd hours, at night and on weekends. The rule here is: leave as little as possible to chance. Remember, many entertainment events take place at night, in various time zones, and weekends are often the busiest.

True Portables

Cellular phones that are truly portable (not just cordless) are a terrific boon to music publicists. With the newest generation of cellular phones, you can call from virtually anywhere: inside buildings, from cars, out in the field, just about any place work takes you. Portables are indispensable when the heat is on and you have to make calls or be reachable. You could be at a stadium show where you have a hundred or more media people to take care of—a frantic, nerve-wracking situation that requires all the technical help you can get.

Airline Phones

Don't overlook this expensive but valuable service on many flights. If you're in transit and need to stay on top of a situation—such as a cover-photo shoot or a touchy interview for network TV—this air-to-ground link can be critical.

Pagers

These tiny instruments can be very important to you when used properly. "Beepers" are now available on a nationwide basis and with a variety of features. "Sky pagers" now have the capability to download text messages straight into a laptop. Voice models will relay a 10-second message to you no matter where you are; digital units will display a telephone number—with area and other codes—keyed in by a caller. Combination models are now available, to take either voice or digital data.

Several models allow you to turn off the beep-tone (if, for example, you're in a symphony hall) and will alert you with a silent buzzing vibration. Like portable phones, beepers give you a real sense of connection in out-of-the-way places. If you're in a position of authority in music PR, you should have one.

Answering Machines

Today, voice mail is preferable, because of its flexibility. If you do choose an answering machine, you should go for a top-quality device that has the capability to be powered on by a distant call—just in case you forget to turn it on before you leave.

TAPE RECORDERS

Mini- and microcassette recorders are mandatory for the briefcase of any music publicist. You'll use them to record verbal notes, your own interviews with artists, complicated company meetings, and dozens of other activities. It's also a very professional touch to have yours on hand during media interviews. More than once, a journalist's recorder has quit in the middle of dialogue. The newest generation of voice-activated machines are desirable—they don't sit there wasting tape during long pauses. This cuts down the danger of running out of tape just at a key moment.

Get yourself a good one (or more than one) and carry along a few spare tapes in both formats, as well as fresh batteries in both AA and AAA sizes. You never know when a writer or remote crew will need one or all of them, and they'll remember this courtesy a long time.

TRANSCRIBERS

If you're doing a lot of material preparation for a major label or PR firm, these machines can save you a lot of time and button-punching. Desktop transcribers come in both mini- and microcassette formats. They have foot-control pedals that enable you to pause, stop, rewind, and play without taking your hands off the keyboard.

OFFICE PLANNERS/ORGANIZERS

There are dozens of organizational tools that can help straighten out your day (or month, or tour). The heavier your client load and the more demanding your schedule gets, the more you'll rely on them.

Dry-erase boards are wall-mounted gems that you can write on with a special marker and erase the material with a paper towel or common eraser. They're available in many sizes, from legal-pad size to "L.A. Billboard." These "idea boards," popular with authors, scriptwriters, and others who frequently have large projects, can be immensely useful—in conjunction with a PC—in mapping out a bio outline, a company history, or the details of a big tour. You can get them blank, ruled, or with weeks and months outlined.

Magnetic boards, commonly called Cadillacs, are wall-mounts that are very helpful in planning a number of projects and for status-tracking. The individual magnetized pieces can be written on or can hold pasted names, dates, and so on. The magnetic clips can then be moved around as projects develop. Again, in conjunction with a PC, Cadillacs are invaluable when you're putting together an entire press kit under deadline. When two dozen items all have to come at the same time, the more organized you are, the fewer costly mistakes you'll make.

SUMMARY

You don't have to amass a lot of expensive digital toys with blinking LEDs. The important point is for you and your office to be connected with up-to-date communication and data-management technology—within your budget. You can bet your next pay check that your competition is hooked up. If you suddenly get a shot at a big story in *Rolling Stone, Vibe, Vanity Fair,* or *E! Entertainment* you'd better be poised to take advantage of the situation and know how to operate most of the above-listed devices. Once you're familiar with them, you'll amaze yourself at what you can accomplish. Besides, it's fun communicating with Tokyo and Paris at 2 A.M.

Russell Shaw, author of *The Netscape Guide to Personal Finance* (Ventana/ Netscape Press) and *The FAQ Writer's Guide* (MIS Press/Henry Holt) recommends these periodicals: *WebWeek, Internet World, Net Guide, Interactive Week,*

Wired, Net Guide, Interactive Week, and *Billboard* magazine's "Enter*Active File" section.

The following list of suggested additional reading was compiled by James T. Bass, co-author of *The Modem Coach* (New Riders Publishing).

Alspach, Ted. *Internet E-Mail Quick Tour: Sending, Receiving, and Managing Your Messages Online*. Ventana Press, 1995. For beginning users.

Branwyn, Gareth, and Sean Carton. *M*O*S*A*I*C Quick Tour: Accessing & Navigating the World Wide Web,* 2nd ed. Ventana Press, 1995. For beginning users; includes 2 3.5-inch HD diskettes with hyperlinked version of Chapter 5 and Ventana's own Mosaic v 2.0.

Branwyn, Gareth, Luke Duncan, Sean Carton, Tom Lichty, Donald Rose, Shannon R. Turlington, and Jan Weingarten. *Internet Roadside Attractions: Sites, Sounds & Scenes Along the Information Superhighway.* Ventana Press, 1995. For beginning to advanced users; includes CD with full text and Ventana's own Mosaic, for Mac or Windows.

Butler, Mark. *How to Use the Internet.* Ziff-Davis Press, 1994. A picture book for new to casual users.

Carton, Sean. *Internet Virtual Worlds Quick Tour MUDs, MOOs & MUSHes: Interactive Games, Conferences & Forums.* Ventana Press, 1995. For beginning users.

December, John. *Presenting JAVA: An Introduction to Java and HotJava.* Sams.net Publishing, 1995 For new to accomplished users.

Eddings, Joshua. *How The Internet Works.* Ziff-Davis Press, 1994. A picture book for new to casual users.

Emery, Vince. *How to Grow Your Business on the Internet.* Coriolis Group Books, 1995. For casual to expert users; includes suggestions of 11 profitable business-es you can start today.

Gardner, James. *Internet Anywhere.* MKS Inc., 1995. For new to accomplished users; includes 30 days free access to Rabbit Network via a toll-free number.

Grimes, Galen. *10 Minute Guide to Netscape for Windows 95.* Que Corporation, 1995. For new or casual users.

Gunn, Angela, and Joe Kraynak. *Plug-n-Play Netscape for Windows.* Sams.net Publishing, 1995. For new to casual users; includes free trial offer (long distance charges may apply) for EarthLink.Net (no signup fee); Netscape, and WinSock.

Hahn, Harley, and Rick Stout. *The Internet Yellow Pages,* 2nd ed. Osborne/ McGraw-Hill, 1995. For *all* Internet users.

Janal, Daniel S. *Online Marketing Handbook: How to Sell, Advertise, Publicize, and Promote Your Products and Services on the Internet and Commercial Online Systems.* Van Nostrand Reinhold, 1995. For accomplished users.

Kehoe, Brendan P. *ZEN and the Art of Internet: A Beginners Guide,* 4th ed. Prentice Hall, 1996. For beginning users.

Kent, Peter. *10 Minute Guide to Internet.* Alpha Books, 1994. For beginning to intermediate users.

LeBlanc, Dee-Ann, and Robert LeBlanc. *Using Eudora.* Que Corporation, 1995. For new to accomplished users.

Lemay, Laura. *Teach Yourself Web Publishing with HTML in 14 Days.* Sams.net Publishing, 1995. For new to accomplished users; includes CD with HTML editing tools for Mac and Windows.

Levine, John R., and Carol Baroudi. *The Internet for Dummies,* 2nd ed. IDG Books, 1995. For beginning to immediate users.

Negroponte, Nicholas. *Being Digital.* Knopf Publishers, 1995. For beginners seeking an overview with a vision.

Randall, Neil. *Teach Yourself the Internet in a Week,* 2nd ed. Sama.net Publishing, 1995. For new to accomplished users.

Rose, Donald. *Internet C*H*A*T Quick Tour: Real-Time Conversations & Communications Online.* Ventana Press, 1995. For beginning users.

Tittel, Ed, and Mark Gaither. *Mecklermedia's Official Internet World 60 Minute Guide to Java.* IDG Books Worldwide, 1995. For casual to accomplished users.

Turlington, Shannon A. *Walking the World Wide Web: Your Personal Guide to the Best of the Web.* Ventana Press, 1995. For beginning to advanced users; includes a CD hyperlinked version of the book and Ventana's own Mosaic.

Wilson, Stephen. *World Wide Web Design Guide.* Hayden Books, 1995. For casual to accomplished users.

PART 4

PUBLICITY AT WORK

14

PLANNING, IMPLEMENTATION, AND FOLLOW-UP

Now that you have a thorough knowledge of basic music publicity tools and practices, it's time to look at the care and grooming of a client—from the day you begin publicity until the campaign is finished.

Whether you're an independent publicist or an artist doing your own promotion, many of your actions will be the same. And PR strategies are pretty similar throughout the success strata, whether your client is a little-known singer-comic, a major rock band with a half-dozen albums, or a freshly signed group that no one's ever heard of before. But other areas of attention will differ, depending on the act and the circumstances. Often the situation will call for lots of ingenuity on your part, and you may find yourself creating solutions or pathways that are unique to one client.

Remember, every client is different. A corporate client may be quiet and thoughtful, or flamboyant and prone to temper tantrums. The same goes for a musical act, which can range from a sober, academic chamber quintet to the loudest, most outrageous metal/pop band—and everything in between. You will have to decide how each client's unique characteristics can be turned into press exposure, while keeping your own ego and personal feelings out of the situation. Some clients are extremely easy to work with and others are quite difficult, even borderline impossible. You have to set your professional limits, and if necessary, seek advice from others you trust.

THE LONG-RANGE PLAN

Starting with a band on the local level, you want to aim for consistency of exposure (hopefully positive) over an ever-expanding radius. As the act matures and begins playing on a regional basis, the media attention should expand accordingly. The timing here will vary from one band to another, since some may skyrocket while others may remain on a regional level for a long time.

By the time a recording contract is reached, the act should be poised to get a least a small amount of national press. And, professionally handled, this should increase significantly when the first recorded product comes out, normally in conjunction with touring.

Until an act reaches true star status, they need all the positive exposure they can get, in the majority of cases. Once an act nears the top, then the exposure tides turn for the publicist. At this point the situation becomes one of deciding what venues and what timing are correct for the client.

The plan for an act at this level will have to account for periods of heavy activity and for lulls, sometimes long ones between CDs and touring. This plateau of a band's career calls for more "care and grooming" and thoughtful decisions than it does for downright creativity on the publicist's part. Keeping a platinum act's PR plan going in a straight line, though, is still a challenging, demanding task.

What follows are step-by-step approaches for a few sample clients. They illustrate the real mechanics of the publicity process and help serve as food for thought for your particular situation, even if you're a band member or artist handling your own promotion. Some of these steps are very similar to the material preparation and research techniques already discussed, but for the sake of accuracy the possible overlap is unavoidable. (More specifics on handling clients are covered in Chapter 15.)

HANDLING A NEW ACT

Many music publicists find working with a new band the most exciting challenge of all. The band members will most likely be eager to learn, ready to work hard, and, in an artistic sense, hungry.

The following passages assume that the act is playing on a regular basis, at least locally.

Research

New bands or solo artists will most likely have had very little or no previous press. However, you still need to learn as much as possible about them in a short time. If you are the one who's creating materials for them, that in itself is the best education process. If materials already exist, get your hands on them right away—and that includes rough drafts of bios. Check to see if there are any articles in local, college, or even high school newspapers that concern the act. At this point you need every scrap of information that you can scare up. Do your best to overlook nothing—you never know when some little item may turn into a story angle. Carefully study, and take notes on, every bit that you uncover. What you're doing is assembling an overall mental picture of the act.

Locate every piece of recorded material that relates to the act: old demos, unfinished studio tracks, anything. Listen carefully and take notes. More than one music publicist has put all the recorded material into cassette form and listened to it in the car, an excellent way to familiarize yourself with the band in a hurry.

Meet the band, either by phone or preferably in person. If it's humanly possible, catch a live show and/or visit one or more studio sessions. Take note of the musical style, the various members' personalities, and anything that strikes you about the band—personality quirks, a member's penchant for humor, who's talkative and who's not. During this stage, you should be part journalist and part mental vacuum cleaner. This will pay off later.

Talk to the members and manager about publicity and answer questions about your role. If you don't know something, or haven't mapped it out yet, say so. Ask if any members have problems doing interviews. If so, make a note and work on that as the media plan progresses, before any interviews are scheduled.

Formulating the Media Plan

A sharp mental picture of the act should be coming into focus by this time. Your next move is to sit down and start thinking in terms of potential exposure for the act—where do they fit? Also keep in mind the question of what is reasonable, given the act and its status. Don't be afraid to be ambitious, but don't set your sights so high that you're crushed when the band fails to get the cover of the local entertainment section right away.

If you're working in a publicity office, you may want to sit down with other publicists in your department at this point and ask for any ideas. Just about any experienced press agent will identify with your situation and take a few minutes to give some tips. If you're a one-person company and going it alone, don't despair. You can start from scratch and still get a respectable amount of exposure for your client.

Start combing through your media list and taking notes on possible targets. With a brand-new act, do not rule out any media outlet, even the smallest and most esoteric. If there's no media list to work from, start locally and go from there. The same goes for the client's media materials. If the client has none, or if they're out of date or not done to professional standards, get going on them immediately. You can't make any real moves, other than planning, until you have pro-level materials on the act.

If it gets you going faster, do the obvious entries on your media "wish list" first (some publicists prefer the opposite). For a rock band, single out the local music columnists, radio and TV "nightlife" correspondents, and entertainment calendars (print versions are good photo targets; electronic ones are good for name exposure). Look for college and high school press in the area, as well as alternative, underground, and specialty publications (charity newsletters or beer-company entertainment sheets, for example). All of these are possibilities.

Read, watch, and listen to the people you intend to contact. If a local TV "nightlife" reporter only does established acts around town, then that person most likely won't take your call about a new band. Conversely, you'll probably find one or more writers and electronic reporters who delight in new bands—to the exclusion of everyone else. College radio and print are a goldmine here.

Keep checking that media list. If it doesn't show that it's been updated recently, you'd better double-check before you go to the next stage. This may sound like a lot of trouble, but do it. There is a lot of turnover in the mass media.

Continue tailoring your target or wish list. You want to avoid sending material on an Amazon power-pop band to a hard-core country-music writer. It's impossible to draw neat lines of demarcation here—the pop-music world is too diverse—but at least think twice about your entries. Look for patterns in media people's work. Some writers and editors are more musically open-minded than others. Look for publications and radio/TV shows that target the same audience as the music of your client.

Begin a list of "angles" about your client that may interest media outlets of various kinds. Good journalistic detective work on your part will pay off here.

Here's a quick shopping list of angles you may glean from a new band:

- Charity work

- Large draws at local clubs

- Antics of devoted fans

- Unusual equipment or stage show

- Musical style or lyrics that are really different

- Interesting and different lifestyles, backgrounds, or education of band members

- Amusing or disturbing anecdotes about group formation or early rehearsals

- Interesting formative bands of various members

This list is virtually endless. Don't let the members tell you, "We're new, we have nothing to say." Keep digging, all the way back to their childhoods.

It's not too early at this stage to start thinking about modest feature story ideas on the act. Neighborhood newspapers and other modest-budget publications in the various members' hometowns are good targets. A nice angle is "hometown boy/girl makes good."

Deciding What to Send

A lot of the exposure that a new act generates is going to revolve around live shows. The other interesting angles you dig up are PR gravy and a testament to your cleverness.

The majority of your mail-outs will consist of a pitch letter and a standard press kit. Remember, though, about tailoring your package for non-music-video TV. For entertainment calendars in print media, draw up a simple form letter with the act name, venue, and date; send this along with photos only—bios and other material are useless to calendar editors. For radio entertainment calendar shows, send only a one-page "entry" with act name, venue, date and (optional) one or two sentences about the act, along with the fact sheet. Send a TV-type kit to television stations that have entertainment calendars within the news or other local shows.

First-class mail is normally okay for these packages. However, if you came into the situation late and the band has an important gig soon, you may have to take more drastic measures. You can "overnight" material to key media outlets. In extreme cases, you might call music critics in your area and just be up-front. Say that it's too late to send material, but you wanted to make sure they've been invited to the show. Explain that new materials will be on hand at the gig. This kind of situation does happen, and most seasoned music writers will understand. Some of them may already have commitments, but at least you have established that first contact. Also, most media people will appreciate your frankness and remember the courtesy.

Other Angles

Think about various aspects of the act and how they might fit into local media as out-of-the-ordinary stories. Could there be a business article on financing their equipment? Do the members all have 3.0 academic averages? Also, various writers around the country love to key in on exciting new bands before anyone else —if the act is really causing a stir locally. Find them by reading every scrap of pop-music press that you can find.

First Followup

After a few days, call music/entertainment editors and free-lance writers to make sure the material arrived intact. Be brief and issue an invitation to the show. Don't expect an answer right then from many media people. If they're coming, they'll contact you in many cases. The important point is not to be overly pushy. Any editor or journalist knows exactly what's going on and what you're up to.

Keep your responses organized. They are the beginnings of your exposure roadmap for the act. If an editor says, "I want to think about it, call me next week," make a note and do just that. Make certain that all press coming to a live show are treated professionally, with tickets at the door, adequate seats, and a couple of drink tickets if applicable.

Second Followup

After a live show and/or interview session with the band, or a contract-signing party or similar event where some press is involved, it's time to make courtesy calls. Check in with writers and electronic reporters to see if they got all they needed. Are there any last-minute questions? Would other photos help, or follow-up phone conversations with act members? Be succinct and end by saying you're available for any last-minute details. The key here is to be helpful, not overbearing.

Tips
Don't push your luck by asking local media people to send you clips—go get them yourself. It's okay to ask media people from other cities, such as nearby college towns, to send a copy of their stories and columns. But if a writer balks, drop it and make other arrangements to get the copy.

After this initial foray into the world of press, any advance or coup concerning the act is more fodder for the media mill: signing a label deal, the opening slot on a concert tour, civic/music/education awards, unusual or funny exploits on the road, or human-interest angles (getting to meet a great musical influence at a faraway gig, for example).

Summary
These steps will get you moving on a plan of media exposure for your brand new act regardless of style or pursuit. Properly followed, these actions will also create a favorable mood locally toward the act. You can use this momentum to reel in other press coverage as the band's musical and touring horizons broaden.

Don't be dismayed by setbacks and other new-band-type hassles. Every new act goes through them. Try to keep a handle on the band's persona and do your best to help management with problems. Stay in touch and keep abreast of developments—you never know when one is ready-made for media coverage in one way or another.

HANDLING A REGIONAL ACT
Your first steps here will be the same as for a new act. Learn the client, thoroughly and quickly.

Research
At this level there's going to be more material to study, such as musical, anecdotal, and previous press. So dig in and take plenty of notes. Gather all existing press-kit material and see what's useful, if anything at all. If there's going to be a total overhaul—which is often the case—get cracking on that right away.

Sit down with management and bandleaders and find out about career plans: touring, recording, label contracts, and so on. If the act already has a label deal and you're an independent publicist, contact the label PR person right away. Offer cooperation in any way that you can. Arrange a meeting with the record-company PR person as soon as possible. He or she will most likely be overworked and will welcome your help. If the inverse is true—you're label PR and the band has an indie PR person, even part-time or family—meet with that person and swap ideas. Again, the keynote is cooperation.

Advanced Research

Find every piece of previous press on the act and study it carefully. Look for trends, both positive and negative, and keep notations of them. This will help you spot press avenues worthy of exploitation—and trouble spots to work on, perhaps in conjunction with management.

Go to a couple of gigs—perhaps inviting a few press people along the way—and observe the act. Get to know the members and crew on a professional basis. When possible, sit in on a couple of interviews and watch while taking your own notes. Later, ask if the members have any questions about interview etiquette. Make a list of any bad habits that you observe, and later sit down with members and management to discuss them. For example, members who hit on female journalists or who've had too much to drink during interviews just don't cut it anymore.

Be sure to compliment the members on correct things they do, onstage and in interviews, but do it sincerely. If questioned, explain that you're there to help in a professional capacity, and give a thumbnail explanation of what PR is all about.

Formulating the Media Plan

Here your initial wish-list should range far and wide, throughout the region. And no matter where you're located, there's going to be a lot of media in a tri- or quad-state area. Begin with the same parameters as for a new act: where do the band and their music fit?

Get your media list updated and expanded. With a band of this level, you'll have considerably more ammunition to work with. Start a multilevel plan that includes, but is not limited to:

- Straight-ahead touring press to coincide with live dates

- Possible feature-story ideas and target outlets

- Columns that you want to supply with tidbits

- National venues—such as columns—that you want to pursue

- Specialized press—trade, tech, business, arts—that you want to broach

Depending on the act or other type of client, your list is going to vary widely. Put some real thought into it; don't be timid about at least considering the bigger game like newspaper entertainment feature stories and national music magazines, as well as really out-of-the way venues like college literary/arts magazines. Remember, every event or occurrence is a possible shot at press for the client. The trick is determining what you can do with each one and proceeding logically.

Deciding What to Send

This stage will be much the same as for a new band, except more complex in the types of packages and their targets. For a regional band, be very careful about old PR materials. Don't send out photos that have already appeared in various media. Also, get all the other press-kit components updated first.

A lot of your send-outs will be the standard press kit, but others will require expert tailoring. If you're pitching a feature story to a regional, city, or specialty magazine, include a few more clips and one or two more black-and-white photos. Follow the TV rules for any local stations that you're approaching.

If you already have some good contacts within the media, call them and briefly let them know you're now on the case for your act. Sometimes this produces surprising results in the form of immediate requests for interviews.

Other Angles

Keep in mind that with a regional act that's been gigging around for a while, there's going to be more PR ammunition. It's your job to get in there and find it. Then figure out how best to use it. Just remember the criteria: interesting things to an editor or producer—and hence the reading/viewing public.

Some items might be a string of record-breaking crowds at area clubs; a restored equipment truck; human-interest tidbits such as a freebie show at an orphanage; unusual guitars or other gear; new technology in the studio or on the road (using a laptop to send tour information back and forth from the home office, for example). The only limits here are your imagination and your knowledge of the media.

First Followup

This key step is virtually the same as for a new client. As usual, turn up the blue flame on any special requests (at least those that are reasonable). These may include extra photos, CD copies, or an extra pair of tickets here and there.

Second Followup

Although essentially the same procedure as for a new act, this stage is going to be more demanding on your part—more people to contact and more last-minute details to iron out. Stay with it, even if this keeps you in your office till 10 P.M. Never assume anything; double-check instead. But don't overdo it and call a writer or editor six or seven times with trivial questions. Once is normally enough after the event, unless there are special circumstances such as a major feature story being planned. Journalists will often call you if they need something at the last minute, but most media people appreciate the feeling that you're staying right on top of things. That part is amazingly easy—just a couple of phone calls per publication or station.

The keynote during this phase is *be reachable* when stories are going to press and electronic appearances are being planned. Fact-checking and additional information can be critical to a given story.

Tips

Keep a close tie-in with media people who've been favorable to the band. They may continue this treatment, so a little extra attention is quite ethical and can pay off in the continuum of the act's coverage. If a college writer from a nearby university town is coming to your city, take that person to a nice dinner. Extra tickets, rare T-shirts, copies of rare early EPs, and similar thoughtful items go a long way to keeping good relations with media people. Also, you never know when that local beat-writer is going to move upward to *People, down beat,* or *Ebony.*

Summary

Working a regional band can be really exciting and challenging. The main point is that you are an important cog in the machinery of their career-building. Be mindful of that and don't miss exposure opportunities. Be ready if the band blows wide open and jumps to the national level.

HANDLING AN ESTABLISHED ACT

If you stay in music publicity, it won't be long before you find yourself involved in a project with a real "name" act or even a genuine superstar band. Remember: as the level of the client goes up, so do the intensity of pressure, the subtlety of temptations, and the critical nature of errors, both of omission and commission.

Life at this plateau can be tremendously exciting, but keep your wits about you. You'll discover soon that the people involved are just humans, like everyone else. Don't let the pressure (real and imagined), the egos, the petty power trips, and the thunder-stealers turn your dream gig into a nightmare.

Research

At this stage there's going to be a ton of previous press to read and you need to digest all of it, taking notes along the way. The same goes for the client's musical library. It may be so massive that you have to listen to it in stages, but do it. If you represent a real superstar act with numerous multiplatinum records, you need to be ready to answer a question from Radio Luxembourg about a track on a 1993 CD.

Advanced Research

Again, look for patterns in the coverage, but with even more scrutiny than for the new and regional acts. Do journalists consistently hone in on the guitar work, or the beauty of the lead singer? Does the group's huge touring entourage get lots of attention? Has there been a notable inconsistency in the musical product (hit album, flop album)? The possibilities can go on ad infinitum, but draw that mental picture. It'll help you make future decisions and handle situations.

When possible, match these patterns with points about the act that you may discover are not addressed. This is the stamp of a good publicist.

Listen to the new product until you know it backward. Study the new PR materials (if ready) until you can recite them by heart. Red-ink any errors you discover in the printed materials. Pick apart the new bio—you may have to overhaul it in as short a time as a month if the bass player quits.

You may have to do all this homework on the run if you've been hired at the last minute and the tour begins on the following Monday. In that case, form a study plan and try to stick to it. Don't rationalize away the need to know the act thoroughly by saying, "I'm too busy with current stuff."

Talk to a few of your journalist contacts. This can be very revealing about the act and its previous PR affairs.

Look at existing interview/TV footage. If you notice any problems, take notes and consult with management. If you discover serious problems, you may need to hire a media coach.

TV Tips: Begin with the basics—don't fidget; maintain eye contact with the host or hostess; keep gestures to within about 18 inches of the torso; don't look at the camera; and keep answers short and concise.

Formulating the Media Plan

Chances are your label or firm will have an extensive national and international media list. If you feel that yours is weak or out of date, check with your colleague at the independent PR firm, label, or management office, whichever is the case. That list must be updated before an ounce of mail goes out, if you're going to do justice to a platinum act.

Start your target list when the main media list is complete, or work simultaneously. If a big tour is about to begin, or is already in progress, work up the most imminent dates first and then outward to the end of the tour. This will take a little pressure off you. You may have to handle the nearest dates moment by moment for a week or so until you can get caught up.

Depending on the size of your office, you may be doing only one sector of the act's media, such as tour publicity or national publications. If you're an independent hired to augment a really monstrous tour, you want to be on top of each segment, helping when possible. Cooperation here is vital between label, indie, and management.

Do not let communication wires get crossed at this level. If things are really humming, suggest a daily phone conference with you and your counterpart at the label or PR firm.

Here's one excellent way to get the media plan into high gear in a hurry: you and your counterpart compare notes and then work as a team on your respective best contacts around the country, both for tour press and for bigger game like TV, national feature stories, key album reviews in major music publications, and so on. Teamwork can turn a national campaign red-hot in terms of coverage. Brag later about who got what, and stay in touch hourly if necessary. Use all of your technology to stay organized and keep things running efficiently.

If you are working as a team, and you're not the sole PR contact, freely make your media contacts aware of the other person. Trying to shortcut, ignore, or steal the thunder of the other PR person will only lead to industrial-grade trouble. If the other person is trying to do this to you, emphasize teamwork first. If that doesn't work, go over that person's head. Infighting can wreck a national campaign.

As the campaign begins to settle down and run smoothly, begin addressing the ancillary or secondary press: specialty magazines, general-interest publications, talk shows that don't normally deal with pop music, and dozens of other outlets you may figure out.

Depending on the act, your office may be swamped with requests from various media even before your materials go out. Consider each of these, of course, carefully. Don't make snap judgments on big media requests. If it's a national magazine or TV network, tell them you want to consult with management and you'll get right back to them.

Certain publications, TV and radio shows, and particular writers may do a hatchet job on your client just as a matter of routine. Know these danger zones and, if possible, keep the act away from them. This can be a *very* touchy area. If you turn down a major venue, you can create waves of backlash, but you may have to take that risk if the resulting coverage is almost certainly going to be bad for your client.

Dictating terms to media outlets has recently become trendy for some PR people who have clients with enough "name clout." This is a very dangerous game for music PR people, especially if unreasonable demands are made. If you hold a national editor's toes to the fire with one major client, that same editor may very well stab you with a long knife down the road. You may not always have that high-power client. And you'll need a job and lots of exposure next year.

It's not that difficult to decide what's reasonable with a superstar client. Demanding veto power on copy and photos is a dangerous ploy. On the other hand, negotiating for cover stories featuring your star client is perfectly ethical. In short, playing games with national editors (or any journalist, for that matter) is not a wise pursuit.

As your media plan takes shape, remember the old axiom and strike while the iron's hot. Do not overlook or callously blow off secondary opportunities for your client. Normally the danger of overexposure for your act is going to be slim unless the band is one of the top five worldwide.

Deciding What to Send

Overall, this is easy for a name act. The majority of your mail-outs will be the standard press kit. Keep the TV rules in mind and augment TV paks with videotape. For the really big game—the top prestige publications and radio/TV network shows as well as seminal overseas media—exercise your brain-power in tailoring the package. For a graphically elegant magazine like *Vanity Fair*, you'll want to include your most striking photos, and of course the promise of originals. For the BBC, you may want to offer rare studio outtakes and exclusive interview tapes to fatten up a special on your act. Serious thought is the key to tailoring a pitch-package.

For a superstar act, many of these decisions will be made for you: a lot of media outlets will call you first and tell you what they want to see.

Other Angles

With a hot act, other angles are like pebbles on the beach. Don't be alarmed if you wake up in the middle of the night and reach for pen and notepad (the sign of a music publicist in overdrive—the same as answering your phone at home on weekends, "Publicity. . ."). Go past the obvious and remember the often-overlooked areas: charity/human interest; technical; hobby/nonmusic interests; civic/humanitarian awards; industry input/contribution. With any major national act, these will keep you busy six days a week. If you want to work seven days, spend the seventh talking to overseas label reps, asking how you can help in their country.

Stay on top of your act's Web activity and Newsgroup scene. Log on at least once a day, preferably more often. Feed your ideas and input to the Webmaster on a consistent basis.

First Followup

It's the same as with other levels. Keep checking to make sure things arrived safely. If necessary, have assistants and interns help with this—but keep the big guns on your list. Checking in with weekly newspaper entertainment editors is good experience for interns.

Second Followup

Again, this is crucial on a national level. Feature stories and network appearance can get incredibly complicated. Use all the available new tools and keep on top of your big stories. After the fact, send thank-you notes and, in particular situations, special (legal and ethical) goodies to those who do a good job for your client. Taste and ingenuity help here: L'Amy pens, digital pocket "phone books," and so on.

Tips

On a national level, leads and favors to media people who don't directly concern your client can be a big image-booster for you. You may come across a little item that could be of interest to a particular writer or producer. Take the time and alert that person. Believe it, he or she will remember this, even subconsciously, and give your clients better treatment the next time around. Many, many cover stories and other important treatments have been decided on just this basis. Do not, however, involve yourself in controversial issues.

Summary

The biggest and most complicated international campaign is not an impossible task. Keep this in mind and, if needed, don't hesitate to hire carefully chosen outside specialists.

HANDLING A PROBLEM ACT

Good PR, even a well-oiled, high-powered campaign, is not a cure-all for a group that has problems. You need to understand this with a new client or at the outset of an assignment—and keep it in mind at all times. You cannot hope to solve all of a band's problems, so don't even try. What you can do is take a serious look at the act from a media perspective and that's where you, the press agent, fit in.

Don't let others delude you, and don't delude yourself that an act with a history of bad press or no press at all can be turned around quickly or easily.

Some of the problems may very well have come from previous PR departments or indies. Isolate those right away, because those headaches need to be halted and rethought as a first priority. It may be helpful to talk with a few writers and editors that you know around the country. Most of the time, veteran music critics will be straight with you and tell you about past problems with the band.

Often the cause may be trouble within the band, touring, the recording process, or management. Such problems, however subtle, may have generated bad ink or, even worse, caused the act to be summarily dismissed by the media. Managers and musicians of all kinds often try to solve problems by playing "presto change-o." This almost never works, unless the moves are very carefully thought out. A problem band can't just sign a new label, agency, or PR firm and think the problem will go away.

Put real solutions in writing; isolate as best you can the past mistakes of band, management, label, and PR firm. Stay within the realm of what you believe you can solve. If the situation is completely out of control, steer clear. The act will no doubt dissipate soon—and take a lot of people with it. This may sound cold-blooded, but keep your eyes open. When possible, have serious, in-depth consultations with management and label brass.

Tips

- Start with the label, then management. If they're not willing to listen, you're stuck. If there is no effort to change things, consider leaving for other pastures.

- On the media end of the act, consider hiring a professional coach/consultant to improve members' performance during interviews or on camera.

- Take severe measures if necessary: isolate problem members from the press; isolate and fire management or crew troublemakers who've messed up interviews because of some personal vendetta.

- Consider a complete overhaul of the act's media plan: all new materials; an interview lock-down for a period while things are sorted out; costume and materials changes to suit the act better media-wise; extensive meetings with individual members to help isolate and define the problem.

- If you sense impending disaster—such as a big drug bust or label bankruptcy, take your things and get out. There are always work opportunities elsewhere. It is imperative to keep your good reputation.

SUMMARY

National music PR must coincide with an overall career plan. Properly done, your PR plan will help the act to "sell-thru"— in other words, achieve maximum sales and career longevity. This is a real career feather in your cap—and word gets around.

15

DAY·TO·DAY SURVIVAL

In the classic cult film *Repo Man,* Harry Dean Stanton remarks with his inimitable dry style, "The life of a repo man is always intense." The daily life of a professional music publicist may not be *that* intense, but it is almost never boring or routine.

This chapter is a grab bag of tips, trouble savers, problem solvers, and survival secrets. If you wake up one morning inside music PR, what follows will help you avoid the feeling that Larry L. King described so accurately in *None But a Blockhead,* in a scenario about a tense negotiation session in a New York skyscraper: "Carnivorous creatures waited down below, open-jawed and dripping. . . ."

THE GIG SHEET

The gig sheet is a roadmap of your client's media plans for a given city on one day. It is an extremely important organization device, whether it is on a legal pad or computer file.

Your gig sheets are worked up from the *master itinerary log* of each client. Your master itinerary should be laid out calendar-style, with the days of the month. Normally the client's booking agency updates this information on a regular basis. If you're using paper, make your entries in pencil so that cancellations and replacement dates can be entered easily.

Keep your gig sheets separated by client so they can be referred to at a moment's notice. The media information that you enter is gathered from your office's media list and/or your reference materials. Enter only one day's plans per sheet to avoid possible confusion (some cities may take more than one page). You want the gig sheet to hold every piece of information you may need as that show draws nearer—right up to that day and afterward. The gig sheet is also useful for followup and for planning future tours. Take the time to keep your gig sheets up to date. They're lifesavers when things are frantic in the middle of a tour.

Following is a sample blank gig sheet. You can customize your gig sheets to suit your taste. After you gain a little experience, you might incorporate your gig sheets into a PC database program.

PROJECT

Client:

Date: Hall: Phone:

Band Hotel: Phone:

Other info (location of press party, banquet, etc.):

MEDIA INFORMATION (pertinent information about each media outlet that you plan to contact; leave room for notations):

Name (editor, producer, or other contact person):

Phone: Fax:

Outlet (publication, radio station, etc.):

Address: Room/Suite Number:

City/Zip:

Material sent (date, type of material):

Calls (enter dates here):

Disposition (note how each editor reacts on a given day):

Writer assigned: Phone:

Other notes:

Name:

Phone: Fax:

Outlet:

Address: Room/Suite Number:

City/Zip:

Material sent:

Calls:

Disposition:

Writer assigned:

Other notes:

LEAD TIME

"Lead time"—the period between the planning of a publication or show and the time when it actually appears or takes place—is very important. If you send your pitch letters and kits too early, they may be put aside and forgotten. If the material's too late, you've wasted your time and expense.

Here are some guidelines for various lead times:

- Newspapers: three to four weeks in advance of publication date

- Radio/TV talk shows: four to six weeks in advance of local appearance (if possible)

- Magazines: months in advance of publication date, so send out new material as soon as it's ready; for music publications, get advance material (tapes, bios) out quickly, since music/entertainment magazines like to time their stories with the new CD release and tour openers. (See the Alan Light interview on pages 147–151 for more.)

CRISIS SITUATIONS

Crisis situations don't occur all that often in music PR, but they are certainly a possibility. For example, you could be hit with a news investigation on payola, dope, or some other music-business scandal. If so, keep your cool.

What follows is an exaggerated example of a phone query, but you should be ready for similar situations:

"This is John Doe with X-Network News. We're putting together a feature on corruption in the music business. Sources tell us that your label president gave large amounts of cocaine to XXX band in return for a contract. Can you confirm this?"

Be very, very careful how you phrase your answer. Good investigative journalists can articulate questions in such a way that virtually any response may give something away.

Keep this in mind: you don't have to answer a leading question from a journalist, no matter how threatening the circumstance may seem. Hard-news reporters don't care how much pressure they level on people. If you are completely thrown by the question and if you sense trouble, give a "canned" evasive response such as:

"I can't respond to that question at this time. I'll have to check with management and call you back."

"I'm sorry, I have no comment."

If the questions are of a serious nature and you want time to think, tell the caller you'll get right back to him or her. If it's a breaking news story that somehow involves your client, you may very well want to consult with your PR or division boss—or the label president and/or act management. Alert the concerned people in your company right away and, if necessary, have a quick meeting to decide your response.

PRESS CONFERENCES

At some point you may also get good news, something that you consider exciting about your client. How to properly handle this information requires putting on the thinking cap. Unless your data is of truly earth-shaking consequence, resist the urge to call a news conference. More than one excited music publicist has announced one, only to have media people go away, angrily shaking their heads because the item wasn't important enough for them to go to all that trouble. Consult with your division heads and client management before making a decision on a news conference, even if it's a major international tour by a reclusive superstar act. You may be truly excited, but the event could be something that's more efficiently handled via phone calls and quick press releases.

A DAY IN THE LIFE

The music publicist's day might start out in a variety of ways. If you have a big tour underway, you may have several urgent phone calls to return right away. This will dictate the pace of the whole day, and the better organized you are, the cleaner you'll get through it. There also may be numerous e-mail messages to sort and respond to. You may, however, be in a less hectic period—for example, the planning stage, before a tour actually begins. In that case you'll spend the morning organizing between phone calls and e-mail.

If you have a few minutes when you arrive at the office, spend them "taking stock" of the day as you sip your first cup of coffee. A legal-size "Do It Today" pad is very handy for this, but don't enter anything else on that pad. Electronic notebooks are also handy for this and other organizational tasks. Look through your mail and separate it into different bins: urgent, pay attention, later, maybe, and trash. Read and file the day's clippings on your clients.

Later in the morning you'll probably be working up gig sheets for an upcoming tour, or putting together materials to "service" the tour. When sending out these materials, you'll need to make several decisions on lead times.

If you've done your preparation homework, a lot of your late morning may also consist of getting calls from the media. These will be positive responses or editors/writers wanting interviews with your client—or better, wanting to plan feature stories or guest appearances. This is the real PR gravy train for the music publicist. In these cases, you will take down the information and arrange any requests for more material like color slides, bios, and so on. Pay special attention to these requests: every editor believes that his or her publication is special and will appreciate your willingness to "overnight" added material.

In the prenoon hour, you may need to relay your interview information to the band's assistant manager or road manager. For key interviews and special situations, you might have to clear this data with the manager via phone, e-mail, or fax. A good line of communication between you, the manager, and the designated road person is imperative.

After lunch, if there's a lull in touring, your office may be quiet enough to do some catch-up work. This may involve reading trade papers, filing materials, working on a bio outline, or putting together a client's activity report (calls, mailings and other work on their behalf, detailing potential stories). There may also be time for important correspondence, including thank-you notes. These notes may seem trivial in light of your other demands, but they're quite important in the proper setting. An editor or writer who's gone to a lot of trouble and done a good piece—even an objective piece that has some criticism in it—will always appreciate a short note saying, "Good story!" or just "Thanks." Media people have egos, too.

There may be time to log on and visit your company's Web site to check on your clients. You might also sit in on a short meeting with your label's Webmaster to help plan that night's updates—or a complete overhaul, with all-new bio material, video, and sound.

Or the afternoon may be frantic with action—especially if there's a big tour underway—with calls coming in faster than you can take them. The fate of a magazine story or major newspaper's concert review may ride on one of these phone calls, so make certain to return them ASAP.

If an office assistant or secretary is helping take the phone load, make sure the information on the call slips is accurate, including the time. When a truly urgent call comes in, don't hesitate to tell the truth to the person you're speaking with: if the conversation isn't critical, tell the person you'll call them back. Journalists will understand—the same thing happens to them. It may be necessary to do some nimble line-jumping: punch into line three, tell them you're on the way, and then hop back to line one. Don't get into such a tizzy, though, that you cut people off.

As the office closes and the switchboard grows dark, attend to any last-minute calls that may come from the opposite coast. Make entries in your "Do It Today" pad for the next day. If your evening schedule isn't hectic, you may want to take this time just to sit there quietly and "meditate," or think over problem areas, mistakes of the day, and triumphs of the day. Some really worthwhile ideas and solutions may appear during this twilight thinking—your brain is still humming from the day's schedule. You might take a few moments to read a chapter in your current high-tech book, as in *Web-Building for Dummies*.

Your work day will probably go on into the night. You may be taking media people and band members to dinner, co-hosting a listening party, or taking care of the press at a show—either a small club or a 20,000-seat hall. You may also be making several stops if more than one of your acts are in town. Dress on the nicer side for whatever occasion, whether a poolside party or a candlelight dinner. Remember, you represent your label, agency, and client. Watch how you act, even if others are howling like wolves on top of the bar.

If the night is really going to be busy, it's a good idea to have along a small PR survival kit, and it doesn't have to be bulky or heavy. Here's a sample checklist:

Alka-Seltzer/aspirin substitute	Pens/notebook
Phone credit card	$2 in quarters
Micro-recorder/batteries/tapes	Penlight
Digital notebook	

If you're going on a "run-out" (overnight junket) to a show, here are some additional items for your briefcase:

Copies of the gig sheets	Hotel confirmation numbers
Two extra press kits	Extra business cards
Extra identification	

At the end of the day, you're back at your hotel room or apartment. Provided you don't have to check in with your office on the other coast, now's the time to kick back and congratulate yourself. You'll most likely have set a lot of exposure wheels in motion over the last sixteen-or-so hours. You can probably go in to the office late, you won't have to punch a time clock, and you won't be doing the same thing the next day.

16

THE PROFESSIONALS TALK

Accurate information and advice from people who work behind the scenes are invaluable to anyone who wants to learn more about the music business. What follows is a collection of interviews with music industry professionals who are outstanding in their respective fields. They offer insights and viewpoints from their positions in PR, management, promotion, new technology and communications, and television. Obviously they don't agree on every issue, but their opinions—taken as a whole—reveal much about the constantly evolving business of music and entertainment.

GILLIAN RENAULT,
Vice President, Public Relations, E! News Daily, E! Entertainment Television, Los Angeles

Let's get a little background.
GR: I was educated in England, where I grew up. I came here when I was twenty and went to California State University at Northridge with an English degree. I didn't go into public relations until I was in my early thirties. I had another two other careers before that. I was a writer and a journalist.

In fact, when I hire people, I always like to bring people in who are good writers, or who have had some journalism background. They understand the mechanics. It is a mindset, how a journalist thinks.

If you understand what an editor thinks, what they need, then you will be more effective. You will not waste time or make people angry with unworkable requests.
GR: Exactly, and you can build a mutual respect that way. If a reporter really knows that you, as a publicist, can always come to him with reasonable, well-

thought-out usable ideas—then even if they cannot use them every time, they will take your calls.

Could we talk for a moment about promotion to television, what television assignment editors need, what kind of materials are useful?
GR: Television assignment editors are radically different from print editors. They have shorter deadlines. Often they will get a call that morning for the four o'clock news show and they rely on visuals to tell their story. So you do have to think differently with them. They tend to use shorter stories conceptually. Whereas with a print editor, you can give a lot of background and the various ramifications of an idea, with a television editor you really need to give them just the top line. What can they fit into a two-minute story that will tell the story very concisely and in a way that is easy for viewers to understand. So I would say that simplification is very important.

For E! Entertainment Television particularly, there is such an appetite out there for entertainment. I think when you see the local news station starting its evening news with a story on a major celebrity, it bears this out. The current interest really started with "Entertainment Tonight," which I also worked on. It was one of my first publicity jobs. It was in 1982, in its second season.

I remember back then stories that people were coming to me wanting to write. How could a half-hour show with nothing but entertainment news survive, much less get big ratings? We now have an entire channel devoted to entertainment news. The field has definitely grown.

On E! Entertainment, how much music are you going with these days?
GR: One of the regulars on our network is David Adelson, who is the editor of *Hits* magazine. He has done many stories for us about the music industry. We like to balance all of our news with the insider's look that we feel consumers will be interested in. He does that for us in music. We include a lot of music coverage. We have our E news daily, which is a half-hour. Music business news is picked up there.

Breaking acts, versus established stars?
GR: The stars are the bread and butter, because people like the familiar, especially with David's input. But we certainly do look for the up-and-comers.

How do you envision and shape your promotion for E! Entertainment? Where do you want presence, trade publication, print and electronic, and so on?
GR: Everywhere.

We think very much alike.
GR: Everyone is touched by entertainment. So we have a very broad-based campaign. I am part of the marketing department. We work daily to increase the

brand awareness of the channel, nationally and internationally. Part of that is the publicity end. Yes, we definitely go to trade papers. We go to the cable trades because that is our business. We go to the Hollywood trades. We find we get less pickup in the music trades. Also consumer press. We go to every outlet we can, from *Entertainment Weekly* to the local newspapers, the *New York Times*. There are too many to list.

Internationally, some examples there?
GR: We actually do less because we are still in very much in the growing mode, internationally. We actually do less consumer publicity internationally. Most of our international push is business-to-business, since we are trying to see to potential buyers of our programming. At this moment, our gossip show is going to be sold in England. There is a publicist over there working for the buyer.

If you could speak briefly about the C Net agreement?
GR: The C Net agreement is very exciting. It includes every element of entertainment—film, television, music, theater. What we have done is create a new company. It is a co-venture between C Net the computer network and E! and this new company. It will create what we hope will become the ultimate entertainment resource online. We have some wonderful graphics. It is http://www. Eonline.com. We are going to use some of the new technology that C Net has.

BARRY NUGENT,
Assignment Editor, E! News Daily,
E! Entertainment Television, Los Angeles

Let's get a little personal background.
BN: I went to the University of Arizona and majored in journalism.

Where did you cut your teeth, and how did you end up in television?
BN: I come from a family of journalists. My father was a journalist for *Newsweek* magazine. For about twenty years he was the bureau chief in Africa. During college I worked at the local NBC affiliate.

You had media experience by the time you got out of school.
BN: That's right. Then I entered the L.A. market.

I like to include a little educational background because many of my readers are either students or interns or just getting into the business. I like a word of encouragement. I did it—you can do it, too. Tell me about your department.
BN: I am the assignment editor for E! News Daily. It covers the world of enter-

tainment from music, television to movies, to literature. We cover it all, if it's entertainment.

Musically, your bread and butter would be the superstars.
BN: That is what we like to do. We like to cover the superstars certainly because they are the most recognizable faces. We are in the business of entertaining people. We want people to tune in and watch us and come back. The way to keep them watching is to bring them the biggest and best stars. So as far as music goes, you really want to bring them the brightest and biggest faces, so they see our channel and see Whitney Houston and they are glued to the set.

In that context, would you on occasion address a breaking act that was really starting to make waves in a region?
BN: Yes, because we do have a news flair in the program. It is E! News Daily, so if there is somebody who is making news some place it is our responsibility to cover it. We would need to make sure that this is not just a flash in the pan but somebody who is here to stay. We do our research when it comes to that. We see what *Billboard* thinks of them. We look for the latest articles on them. We talk to a lot of people before we do some of the smaller acts.

Typically, who would give you the pitch, the publicist?
BN: Yes, a publicist would call. Oftentimes the publicists are not so good in making pitches. I hope I don't offend anyone out there.

No, I want you to tell it straight, please.
BN: It is easy to pitch the big names, right? Whitney Houston, Bruce Springsteen. When you are talking about some of these smaller acts, they think that if they say, "This person is really hot in the South, I am telling you on my word that they are going to be hot." That is just not enough. We need to hear a lot more, yet that's what we hear more than anything from publicists. "These people are great, I am telling you they are really great and they have a lot of backing from people and they are number one on the radio charts here."

They don't give enough inside information. These are small acts and we like to research them and we like to know what is going on and they just don't supply us with some of that information. Often we will just forget about it because there are so many small acts out there. There are only a few we can go after.

So the better prepared the pitch, the more likelihood of attention.
BN: Absolutely—we are in the business of storytelling here. We like to tell a good story. If the publicist tells us a unique story—for instance, "There is a rapper out there and he came from south central and he is blind." It is a sweet story and they are pitching it that way. "It's against all odds and he finally got a recording contract. He has not played much and I don't even know if he is going to

make it as a musician but this kid is pouring out his blood and guts to make it." All of a sudden, you see this is a sweet story. This is a story about somebody who is really trying. It's not half bad. If they pitch it as a story and they tell the story of this person's life and then additionally offer locations. We are a visual medium, so we need to tell the story as visually as possible. A sit-down interview is not enough. Sometimes they'll say, "He will be in the office tomorrow, do you want to do the interview?" No.

You want footage of his Leader Dog or his cane or interacting with people.
BN: Exactly. If he visits hospitals on the side. We want to go to the hospital and we want to know his interests.

I stress this repeatedly—whenever possible, it is better to have a hook beyond the hit record. Charity work is great. Could you walk us through a successful press kit being sent to you? It would have a concise cover letter outlining the points above, an artist bio, 8 x 10 glossy, a video?
BN: A video would be good. We like to go out and shoot our own footage. Obviously, if it is in a rural area or if it is in a place where we do not have affiliates, it is nice to have this footage shot for us. A good press kit should have the glossy, a bio, the music, and a video.

What tape format would be acceptable?
BN: We prefer Beta, which is broadcast-quality. Also, as far as packaging, sometimes we receive press kits with CDs and all that are banged up. Put it in something that is padded or put in a box.

Also, if the press kit has press clippings, that is good to put in, the more credible the article, the better.

On the television end, my motto is sort of access, access, access. The more access I have, the better I can tell the story. I need the publicist to talk to me about those things.

Things have changed dramatically. Everyone covers entertainment news now and that's also part of it. There is so much competition out there. The more unique the story you can pitch to the editor, the better. If you are going to pitch one act to "ET" one way, you better come up with a different angle for E!.

It is going to anger me if I see if "ET" also went motorcycle riding with this artist. Come up with a lot of different angles that you can pitch to different people. Also, the viewer is going to see it on one channel. They'll watch it the first time and the second time they won't.

I recall one instance in the opening stages of an Allman Brothers tour. An independent publicist on the West Coast wanted a group-and-grin situation for everybody, a press conference. My associate and I said, "No. You are writing a recipe for disaster. The L.A. Times *is not going to buy that, nor is* Rolling Stone, *and so on.*

BN: That's right. You nailed it.

Any other tips like that you can think of?
BN: Sometimes, if it is an international act, it is good to compare them to an American act. Before Selena's death they pitched her as the "Latino Madonna." So I thought to myself, the Latino Madonna. I could actually tease it that way. That is what the publicist should be thinking. "The Beatles of Australia." You hear that from time to time. Automatically, this is a larger-scale act.

I also advocate, when possible, send materials ahead overnight. With a big tour about to open, I have found myself in a jam time-wise. Trying to cover the entire West Coast in one weekend. My key contacts appreciated that I went the extra cost.
BN: This sounds like a very useful book.

ANTHONY DECURTIS,
Editorial Director, VH-1, New York

Give us a summary of your title.
AD: Well, I have two titles. One is editorial director and the other is correspondent. The first one is about the kind of editorial function that I play and that's working with people on scripts and trying to figure out what kind of stories we are doing. The correspondent title is for on-air things.

Tell me a little about VH-1. What is its mandate, target audience? What is its philosophy?
AD: The target audience is really what people have been calling MTV graduates. People who are essentially over twenty-five and still interested in music, but who are not necessarily going to be looking to MTV as their main source of information about music—the way people do from probably twelve and into their twenties. It is a more adult audience. There is a feeling that some of the high jinks of MTV are not really appropriate for us.

What is going on in the music business today? As the century turns, how would you characterize the industry?
AD: This is not only true of the music industry, but of the "information culture" in general. Things are really in a state of flux. I do not think that people really know how all the technologies are ultimately going to play out.

Are people really not going to go to record stores anymore, are people really going to get their information from various kinds of online functions? We've seen the recent mergers. For example, I work for Viacom and they own Blockbuster Video, MTV, VH-1, Simon and Schuster. There's a sense that all of these things are somehow supposed to be synergistic, to tie in and work together.

Or take the merger of CNN and Time-Warner. Everybody is trying to cover for what the future is going to bring. The music industry is a big part of that. There is a lot of speculation but certainly not a lot of vision. That is the general feeling that I am getting right now. A lot of sense of audience splintering, various ways of marketing to different audiences. The proliferation of cable channels—and how all of this plays into how you get music to people. This presents a complicated question.

Can you give me an idea of when an act might approach VH-1?
AD: Essentially there are at least two aspects of VH-1. One is video programming, headed by Lee Chestnut. Then we have the news department. There is a certain amount of cooperation between these departments. On the other hand, Lee makes his decisions independently. The news department does things that relate to what VH-1 is showing.

As far as programming is concerned, anybody who has a video and is interested in getting it shown can submit it. The playlist, though, is fairly narrow. That can change, however; things do get on there.

As far as the news department goes, there just has to be a story. And it has to be some sort of music that makes sense for VH-1's audience. If your act is a thrash metal band or a gangsta rapper, it is unlikely to get on to VH-1. That's because it does not really make sense in terms of news coverage for our audience.

Generally, the things we do cover range from pop to rock. Certainly, an interested party could contact me directly. We also have an assignment desk. If someone got in touch with either of us, we certainly would bring up the idea.

Can you describe a successful pitch kit?
AD: The kit could be fairly elaborate. Certainly, if we are unfamiliar with the band, we need to have music. I really encourage letters to be as specific as possible, especially since this is entertainment news. There has to be some sort of "tag." What is specifically interesting about this band at this time, about what they are doing? Is it a benefit of some sort that really has a local resonance?

I encourage people to be forthright. This was true when I was an editor at *Rolling Stone*. I definitely like correspondence that really conveys something. A lot of generalities don't do anybody any good. So much stuff comes in that if I can't get the hang of what is going on, my impulse is to let it go. I am not going to try and make sense out of something that's off the mark.

If somebody makes it clear right at the top—what's up—then they can go on for a bit. That way I can choose to read further or not. You want to make sure that nobody has to read more than the top paragraph to figure out what you are looking for. I think that is really the key. It is a simple point, but often overlooked.

Blues and blues-influenced material is becoming popular. Have you noticed that?

AD: We have done some things. When the Rock and Roll Hall of Fame was opening, we did a lot of programming surrounding that. There were blues sequences in that coverage. It's a fine line, achieving a comfortable fit with our audience.

Your advice to the kids of the world?
AD: Specifically speaking, from the standpoint of being at VH-1, there is a sense of new bands starting out. It doesn't hurt to think visually. Obviously, the main priority for anybody making music should be their music. But try to imagine a visual sense. If you have friends who are into cinema studies, see what they are doing as far as using a camera. It can't hurt to fool around a little bit with video. Increasingly, it is how people find out about music. Video is an important way of getting music across to people.

Beyond that, it is mostly about getting to a point, career-wise. We do have the show "Crossroads." It's little like MTV's "Buzz Bend," where new things get tried—or things that we don't ordinarily program are tried. That is a possible place to go. Then, of course, if the band has something specifically newsworthy they are doing. It could be musical or nonmusical, like a benefit performance. That is certainly something they can keep us in mind for. Lastly, good luck.

RUSSELL SHAW,
Author and Columnist

You are now one of the more widely published freelance writers in North America. Let's get some credentials.
RS: Yes, I have interviewed forty-nine CEOs for Delta's *Sky* magazine and I have a weekly column called "Web Wallet" on the Ziff Davis Internet site. I am a contributing editor at Web Week, a founding member of the Internet Press Guild, and a longtime member of the Society of Professional Journalists. I've been in journalistic publications and have written for *Billboard.* One could say that I cover general business issues, entertainment technical issues, television also. I write about media, technology, business, and marketing. Currently I write a lot about about the Internet and the World Wide Web. Two of my recent books are *Netscape's Guide to Online Investing* (Ventana/Netscape Press) and *The FAQ Writer's Guide* (MIS Press/Henry Holt).

There is a lot of activity in the telecommunication world.
RS: Yes, this conversation happens on the eve of the president signing a telecommunications bill. In terms of the Internet and Web, it has many ramifications. It is going to open up additional bandwidth for speedy cable modems. The frequency that cable television uses is a lot broader than the frequency of, say, telephone lines. Cable modems will be able to move about thirty megabytes of infor-

mation per second—"downstream"—from a website down to an individual in their home or from a newspaper. This opens up exciting possibilities in graphics, audio, and video.

Marilyn Gillen has a really good basic introduction to the Internet, so please talk about the Web.
RS: The Web developed more than twenty years after the Internet. With the development of multimedia applications on computer desktops there was really no way to integrate the graphical nature of some of these files. People wanted to either consult, refer to, or exchange. Then you had the very awkward UNIX protocol, so the Internet exchange, before the Web, was basically pure text.

There had to be a better way to distribute data, and also something to act as a repository for these files, including graphics. That is how the World Wide Web was devised. It was invented by Tim Berners-Lee, a brilliant British scientist who was working in Switzerland. He was working at the European Particle Physics Laboratory in 1989.

When the Web made its debut in the scientific community around 1992, word spread like wildfire. Then in the midnineties, with the advent of friendlier software, Web usage and content grew like crazy—everything from music to automobiles. Also, other Internet services such as the Newsnet /CK/ newsgroups became very popular.

Now the paradigm of the Web is one repository, many places, or many users at once. This, as opposed to: "Send me a photo of your band. . . ." You can post it on your website. Now instead of overnighting photos to thirty journalists at once, anyone can visit the website and download the photo instantly. A website allows a music PR person to post tour itineraries and other interesting tidbits about the band that can be accessed easily.

Let's get a clarification on the many different ways to gain Net and Web access; that can be pretty confusing.
RS: You need the requisite hardware. Then you need a way to get on the Web. One of these, which is recommended for beginners and for people with very special content needs, is a commercial online service. As of this conversation there are five or six of them. Some of them are probably going to last for the foreseeable future and others may go away by the time this book comes out.

Do you want to mention the leading contenders now?
RS: America Online, which is still growing quite quickly, is going to be around for quite a while. It is generally perceived that Compuserve is going to stay around quite a while. The online services, for example, have archived newspaper information that is not yet available on the Web. The archived data can be useful in research for both publicists and journalists.

In mid-decade, we saw the Microsoft Network enter the field. Likely, we'll see a lot of online services evolve into giant websites. These services have always said that the advantage they have over freestanding websites is that they are an aggregation of content.

We'll see more people who want to put up their own website as development tools become more common and easier to use. Small record companies are putting up their own websites, rather than using online services. I see a continual evolution. The services may move away from high subscription fees. Their revenue may be from charging for "links." For example, if a label has a heavy website and they want an added presence on an online service's home page, they pay a fee for that open platform.

How about some discussion of direct Internet access?
RS: Internet Service Providers (ISPs) offer access to the Web by charging a flat fee and allowing unlimited access over a month. There are also limited-access deals.

Now, some of the browser tools are supplied by the ISPs. The two most popular browsers are Microsoft Explorer and Netscape. The ISPs are also bundling e-mail software, such as Eudora Light. Using these tools, you can navigate the Web and utilize the various search engines, such as Yahoo! and HotBot.

I think it would be a fair prediction to say we will see more, easier and probably less-expensive Net/Web software.
RS: Any Web conference that I go to, there's the feeling that to become a real mass medium, the technology has to be transparent—in terms of people not having to worry with it.

In the midnineties, the percentage of American households with Internet access was barely into the double digits. It's perceived by the year 2000 that will be as high as 25 percent.

Where to next?
RS: Somebody reading this book might logically ask, "How is this going to help me publicize my act, my label? Remember, the Web is a visual medium as well as a text medium. If you take a look at the standard elements of a press kit that even predate the Web, you have visual elements, you have photographs, perhaps even a tape of a live performance.

The act's logo.
RS: Even a videotape of a live performance.

Advance tidbits of a new release, an upcoming tour.
RS: The Web can be an extremely efficient distribution platform for all these services. The Web can be many things to publicists, whether they are with major labels or with a garage rock bands or jazz combos in Michigan.

Orchestras, symphonies, and whatever, small to metro.
RS: There are numerous sites on the Web now. By the end of the decade they'll number in the thousands, many being music sites. You can put sound clips on a site that the user can download using a tool like Realaudio.

Added information is also popular, data that you may not get with the CD, interviews with some of the artists, pieces of the video, and in some cases, the entire video.
RS: There is also a technology called "streaming," which allows much faster download times.

It's also very important to promote your website—because of the competition. This brings us to the concept of "links." A link is a highlighted point of reference on the text, or graphic, of your website. With the click of a mouse, it'll take the viewer from one page of the website, or to another site altogether. This is a very important exposure concept—with tie-ins to tour sponsors, even hotel information. Many of the major ticket vendors are putting up websites now.

Choose links wisely. There is an argument: If you put too many links to other sites, you may risk sending people away and they won't come back.

Building a site is becoming easier and less expensive.
RS: Yes. With the latest tools, many people are doing their own—where, not long ago, you had to hire out.

What do you see in the arena of newsgroups?
RS: Newsgroups are a portion of the Internet that predates the Web. They are not on the Web per se. This is a separate, text-only section. There are about fifteen thousand now, but is likely to grow much larger before decade's end. Newsgroups cater to communities with specific interests, whether it is a discussion of early recordings or rare musical instruments.

For example, if there is a radical new music form underground that's coming out of Toronto, say, with just a few fans but growing, there's an application.
RS: Exactly. A PR person should be aware. On most of the Internet services, there are ways to search by key words. If you have a jazz act, just key in the word "jazz." If there are fourteen newsgroups located, what I would do next is what online people call "lurking." Go in, look around. They are all free. Usually they are divided into subject areas called "threads." For example, if there is one named "bebop.fan" you will have several discussions at once. The content varies, from large archives to just a few messages.

It is a publicist's dream come true. A direct link to your most loyal fans.
RS: You're likely to reach opinion leaders—word of mouth is still the most effective way of advertising.

So if your label is about to reissue a blues CD from the late forties then you would need to get in there and find whatever blues clubs, so to speak, and get the word out.

RS: Also, celebrity chats. It is easier to run them through online services than through the Internet. It is a top priority of any publicist to get their act an hour chat session right before a CD ships or before a tour—on America Online or Compuserve.

Clearly, many promotional possibilities here—the bread and butter of any serious publicist.

RS: One thing that I would advise is cross-platform promotion. One should not look at the Web as a substitute for the traditional media—keep all your options in mind.

Russell, how many phone interviews have you done in the last fifteen years, ten thousand?

RS: Quite possibly more, in excess of ten to twelve thousand.

Briefly, telephone technique, communication skills, and maybe some "netiquette." Certain basics: always identify yourself, both ways, if you are the answering or the calling party; speak clearly; don't mumble; try to not drop the telephone, that's really aggravating.

RS: A lot of it is tone of voice.

Some more basics, Russell. Try not to cough into the receiver.

RS: All of it is not necessarily the presentation of the call. Good PR people develop a sense of timing and what's valid. Often the publicist is the last person to know when something happens. A tour is extended, a CD ship date is delayed.

Yes, if you don't know, say so, and tell them you will call them right back and do whatever homework is necessary and straighten it out.

RS: Getting back is very important. Do not put people on hold for indeterminable lengths of time.

Another important thing is backup. When possible, have someone you can depend on when you're out. They should know where you can be reached in an emergency.

These days, in my opinion, it's completely unforgivable not to be reachable. We have bag phones, we have nationwide paging systems. The communication technology is there and you need to learn it and use it.

I've heard stories about people at big outdoor events using bag phones and pagers to stay in contact with each other. Things can get pretty hectic, the larger the event the more crazed it can become. I have had say, probably twenty to twen-

ty-five media people all with needs, demands to stay on top of—before the era of portable phones and pagers and voice mail; it was difficult.

RS: Today, voice mail is an absolute must. Technology is a boon to the professional publicist. Learn it and use it.

ALAN LIGHT
Editor-in-Chief, *Vibe* Magazine, New York

A little personal background, please.

AL: I grew up in Cincinnati and then went to school at Yale, as so many people in the music business did. Then I came here and worked briefly for a magazine called *Seven Days* published by the *Voice*. Then I returned to *Rolling Stone*, where I had interned, and worked there for about five years. I was a senior writer when I left. I came here to help launch this magazine as the music editor in 1993. In 1994 I took over this job.

Please tell us a little about the publication.

AL: Well, the short version is that *Vibe* chronicles urban music and urban culture. The hardest part is the terminology. It still kind of lags behind the way people actually listen to music. It is frustrating sometimes, that "urban" as an industry term is fairly accepted. But outside of that, I feel people out in the real world do not necessarily know what that means.

Here, there's a burden or responsibility, however you see it, to really define an audience that already exists—to try to bring together the different elements that fall under this urban music heading. That is the philosophical foundation for the magazine, the culture that emerged out of hip-hop. It is what we all grew up on. At this point hip-hop has effects. It determines the way a whole generation thinks—not just about music, but about the rest of their lives, the clothes they wear, the movies they make and the movies they see. Also, the music they make that might not, strictly speaking, be a rap record.

Hip-hop has affected the way people construct songs, produce and create music. So hip-hop I see as the lens through which we, and our readers, approach the world. Now aside from hip-hop, obviously we cover R&B and dance music, reggae, dance hall, jazz, and when it seems right, certainly more straight rock or pop. I think this audience is not given enough credit for listening to more than just one kind of music. That approach, from the right perspective, still makes sense for us to review an REM record or a P.J. Harvey record. It's a long-winded answer, because at this point I think the audience is clearly defined.

At what point does the world of jazz fit in?

AL: It does fit in. We have a regular jazz column in the review section. There are jazz features. It is obviously not a leading element of what we do, but certainly we touch on it. I think there is interest. There is so much talk about jazz and hip-hop and kids discovering records their parents were listening to.

I think the great gold mine for us is in R&B at this point. The other music magazines recognize that hip-hop has enough rock. So metal kids and skate kids and surf kids, they'll listen to an Ice Cube record. I was at *Rolling Stone,* writing about a lot about hip-hop for five years. There's a demographic out there, who are really seen as too young, too black, and too disposable, sort of bubblegum for the rock magazines. These are people selling three, five, ten million records and not getting written about. The fans are not getting information from anywhere.

Look at the charts. TLC is going to sell ten million records and still has not gotten a feature in *Rolling Stone* or anywhere else. Art Kelly, Whitney Houston, those are not genre artists, those are multiple-platinum superstars. They are not really getting dealt with anyplace else. I think that is a huge expanse for us to do whatever we want.

If you could expound a moment on the right way to approach your publication?
AL: I think that a clear understanding of what we are doing is important—this includes not limiting yourself too much. I think there are things that come up, but publicists think they're out of hand and shouldn't come to us with them. Who knows what we are going to be looking for.

It's not to say that I should be getting worked on every alternative record that comes out. But it does amaze me, there are things that are not straight-up hip-hop records, but material by black alternative acts, jazz records—things that I had no idea were coming. All of a sudden they're out in the world. And we just think, "Had we known, we would've found something to do with that." It's bringing a clear understanding of what we are trying to do, without excessive preconceptions.

I stress the idea—do your homework, study the publication and try to get a feel for it.
AL: It is not that hard. My music editor is listed very clearly. That is obviously the place to start. It is fine to come to me or somebody else, but use logic. If somebody throws the word "cover" out—for an act that is not Whitney Houston, they are going to turn me off. Let's start with, "We would like to be in the magazine."

Sometimes publicists get overeager. I have been guilty of that. At times you feel like you have to try.
AL: Where else can they go with certain acts? I understand there are a lot of people coming to us who have never had a national magazine to approach before. If they are used to working with fanzines or with, say, smaller black press, we are kind of a different situation.

There has been and will continue to be a real education process between us and the industry we cover. It is a new thing. It has been hard for some of the artists we write about, because they are used to being coddled in a certain way by fanzines, by photo books. All of a sudden, quotes they actually say—we are writing down. Then they get all scared. If we are going to take them seriously, that is what it means.

One has to be aware of the ramifications when you try to make the leap into the national media. That's very good advice.
AL: That understanding is going to take time. From each direction, from the pitch on one end—to what comes out on the other end, here. Artists, labels, and publicists, all of them are used to certain kinds of relationships with publications. Here, it's not like that.

What types of materials do you like to see or would your music editor like to see?
AL: The sooner we can get to the music, the better. I can speak for everybody here. We listen to an awful lot of material. So the music is always going to be the starting point. Videos and photos are fine. But until we can hear it, I don't think there is a whole lot to go with.

That's always a struggle in some ways. I know that urban artists are really scared of bootlegging, scared of circulation advances. We run up against it all the time. Anything that is an anticipated rap record—it's a big fight to be able to hear any music early. That is where you have to build your trust.

It is a double-edged sword, if you want the exposure.
AL: Professional journalists are not involved in bootlegging. So that is where we need to start from, the music. All the rest of it follows after that. I've got to pay attention, though, if a video is getting a lot of response and generating a lot of attention.

The publicists we've built real relationships with, they are the people you learn to trust. These are people who pick up the phone and say, "Watch out for this, because it is a really good record." And we listen. Over the years they've told me when the material is really good, and also when the stuff is not really good, they've been honest. But some oversell everything they get. I understand they are doing their job, but the credibility isn't there. The more honest you are with me, the more I am going to pay attention to you.

Very well put. I also encourage people to give tips, even if it is not your own act or label.
AL: There certainly are some people whom I pay more attention to than others, because they have steered me right.

It is a psychological thing and I'll bet that you would be predisposed to, say, a major feature or even a cover, down the road to said person.

AL: You build those relationships and you see who does have instinct and who has taste. Also, I know this is always hard and it's been hard for me, making the adjustment to a monthly magazine—but being fair, to keep us informed as to release dates changing, it's vital. Nothing turns me off faster than as soon as you have the story locked in, the publicist is gone—and we find out, after the story runs, that the record's been pushed back two months.

That is very unprofessional.
AL: It happens all the time. Sometimes that is in your control and sometimes it is not. Again, it is a question of trust and a respect, to trust us enough to know that if they call and say, "Look, the record has been pushed back a month," they don't feel like they are going to jeopardize a story.

That could make a publicist very nervous, but you have to be professional about it.
AL: At the same time, I do not see that it particularly helps your artist—if the story is off the stands before there is a record out.

It often comes down to a judgment call. What is the professional thing to do in this situation? You have to protect your editors and media people.
AL: There are people who will do that and people who will stay on top of those things and keep us informed. That makes a big difference the next time around.

That's very sound advice. I'm sure that you, like any seasoned editor, have a long memory for both positives and negatives.
AL: Sure. I have made mistakes of my own, mistakes where I listened to somebody and got burned on it's being too late to change it. Even if there is nothing I can do, call and tell me.

I preach, "Think far down the road, not just the moment."
AL: What we've seen over the last ten years, publicists know they can have the upper hand a lot of times. We need artists sometimes more than they need us. Publicists should view magazines more than what we're going to do for them.

You may not always have a superstar act and you may come calling down the road.
AL: It's also important for editors to be realistic and not pretend to be more. I am always the first to say, know MTV can break a record. I don't know if a magazine can break a record. But I think that we are important to the field, where we are the only place that is in a serious way covering a whole culture.

My experience has been careful magazine exposure can really (a) help establish an act, and (b) maintain the longevity of an act. Maybe you cannot break a record, but you are an integral component of a much larger picture.

AL: For example, Prince approached me about doing the first interview he had done in five years. This was a statement that he wanted to come to this audience, he didn't go to *Rolling Stone*. Whitney Houston, the same thing. She could have gone to *Vanity Fair*. We were the only print press she did. It was tremendous, that was a statement. She wanted this audience.

Working with superstars can be touchy.
AL: It is a hard, delicate thing. Superstars are delicate creatures to work with. But creating that trust is the most important thing we can do.

It is refreshing to find you so open, and willing to address so many types of music.
AL: We're still trying to find out all the right balances. Sometimes we will do things and look back and realize that it did not make sense. We are still young. We are still learning a lot about what our readers want or expect of us.

LESLEY PITTS
Vice President of Publicity and Artist Development,
Loose Cannon Records, New York

Let's get a little background on you.
LP: I attended the School of Visual Arts here in New York. I was in a very weird experimental journalism program. It was great because there were no more than ten people in my classes. All of the teachers were professionals in their fields.

I thought I wanted to be Brenda Starr, reporter. Then I found out just how little reporters make. If you started as a publicity assistant, at that time you made a little more. I ended up at Ogilvie and Mather for a couple of years, but I hated it. I found an opening at Columbia Records in corporate affairs. I started out doing special events.

Then I went to a firm called Set to Run, now closed. It was a pretty popular firm and had a lot of rapper acts, R&B, alternative acts. I worked on projects of Ice Cube, Third Base, and did the R&B Foundation Press, plus sundry other rappers. I worked on TLC's first campaign. It was a really good place to learn. You hit the floor running.

You're just in there—sink or swim, right? Then I went to LaFace Records for a brief time. Then I went to Jive Records. There were so many acts on the roster. It was another great learning and growing experience. Moving here was a great opportunity. It gives me a chance not only to do publicity but also to work on image and develop the artist. I'm not just stuck with what I get, as you know, publicists often are.

Tell me how you see yourself, your role now as a publicist and artist development. How do you fit into the overall scheme of an act's career?

LP: I think once a publicist, always a publicist. Actually it is funny, in doing artist development, I miss being able to call in person rather than talk on the phone. I like that.

Every veteran publicist is always subconsciously looking for angles to explore, avenues to open up.

LP: Exactly, and I think that is what I see as my role. Especially the younger artists, who really do not know about this business. I think in the artist development side, my role is a lot of teaching.

On the publicity side, the publicist gets them out there. A lot of times, especially if you are working a label where you are really swamped, it is very hard to come up with new and different ways to do that. That's the challenge to me, to try to find some angle to get them out there. That's why I take by job so seriously, because this is about people's lives and about their careers. I try to do the best I can.

At Capricorn Records in the seventies, we had, among many others, blues singer Delbert McClinton. He was traveling somewhere in Pennsylvania in a station wagon. He opened a candy bar and threw the wrapper out the window. Well, there was a Pennsylvania State Trooper right behind him and he got popped for littering. That was an innocuous enough situation. We took that one item and it appeared in Rolling Stone, *on NBC television, all over. It was just cute enough that it clicked.*

LP: That happens. When I got the TLC project it was one of those things. Who would ever think these girls would sell more records than any girl group ever? The video was out there, no one was really into it. They thought it was just silly. Then one of the girls wore condoms on her eye and her clothes. "In Living Color" did not want them. They wanted them to change their lyrics and they wanted them not to wear the condoms.

I sent out a press release and I'm sure the publicist at "In Living Color" still hates me. I got so much pickup on that and it was not like the worst thing in the world. Certainly those are ways to get your artist out there, new and different ways.

It is possible to overdo it. I have been fortunate in my career that I have never really had something blow up in my face, but I have seen it happen to others.

LP: There's certainly a balance when publicizing an act. You want to get them out there. You want people to know who they are and want to know more about them. You want fans to buy their records and go to see them live. You also don't want them to be overpublicized, overexposed.

You also have to keep in mind that everybody does not want to be a personality, to be a star. It is a very hard balance when you are doing publicity. I had one client who felt like, "I just want people to talk about my music. I don't want them to talk about my life." Once you reach a certain level, that is all people want to know about. They could care less about what it says on your record.

Who is the person dating, have they slipped off to Cannes, or what kind of expensive new sports car or new villa in southern California that no one knows about—it's inevitable.

LP: The best thing is when an artist understands the machine, when they understand how publicity works and how interacting with writers works and they want to be a part of it.

That is when it works real smoothly. My former New York director, Howard Bloom, had a real simple explanation. He would say, look, if people read about you they will be more inclined to buy the record or CD. If the artist is more of a person and a real entity, they are going to buy that piece of music over somebody else. He would say, if we have had a dozen mentions in the last thirty days, fans will be more predisposed to buy the product. Howard was very meticulous about his publicity affairs and he believed in knowing the client thoroughly, interviewing the client extensively, reading all previous clippings, to see how they have been treated, looking for any gaps.

LP: One of the good things about doing artist development, I can see that and say this guy needs a media trainer. This guy needs somebody to teach him how to do an interview, or this person is very shy. These are things that you really need to know before you put an artist in a situation, so that it is fair to everybody.

How much coaching do you do? Say, if you have an act that is ready for a good bit of national exposure, television?

LP: I think it is very important. At a small label like this I can do that with every artist. Again, if it is someone who is younger, they really don't get it. They don't know that you don't have to answer everyone's questions, that if we venture where you don't feel comfortable, you don't have to answer that. They don't know how to take control of the interview. I tell my artists all the time, watch politicians. Watch how they answer questions.

Yes. Something I go on at good length in this book—that there is no such thing as retroactive off-the-record. If you are edging toward an item that might be off-the-record, you better say so first before you answer.

LP: It is always my preference to just not say it.

It is very important, you don't have to answer any particular question if it's too personal or if it is possibly dangerous.

LP: Or you can answer it the way you want. That's why I tell them to watch politicians, ask someone in Congress about their morality issues. They will say, "Well you know, my morality issues aside, I want to talk about X." That's what politicians do.

A nonanswer or answer that is so inane that you know it is not going to end up anyplace as copy.

LP: I don't feel it is my job to scam the media or anything like that. But I also feel sometimes artists are put into the position. It is kind of hard, it is a thin line where they are not comfortable.

Media people differ from one paper to another, from one network to another. Some people have ego problems, as journalists, and have an ax to grind.

LP: Exactly, or they come with a lot of preconceived notions. I remember being in a situation with Ice Cube with writers. Especially with a black act, when they cross over and you get these writers who may not know that much about the genre of music. They come into it with some preconceived items of what a rapper is like. You have to be careful of that because you can come off really badly.

Sure, you stay away from fulfilling any kind of stereotypes. Don't fall into a trap. Most professional media, especially the more experienced ones, they just want to get in there, get an interesting story, and get out. Go on to the next assignment.

LP: That's important. I always tell my artists: read. What interests you, what are you passionate about. Make sure you talk about those things. These days, people want to sit in conference rooms and do interviews. I say no, that is not going to give anybody an interesting story.

You need hobbies, you need charity work, you need things to make for more interesting stories. You are going to get those kind of questions if you keep getting press. The artist needs to understand that any editor or writer, any media outlet, needs interesting material for their readers, viewers, and listeners. Radio talk show for example. They have to keep coming with interesting, intriguing, amusing items.

LP: Outrageous, whatever their personal style is.

One act that comes to mind who were masters at this game is the three guys in ZZ Top. I was fortunate to work with them, back when they were first moving to the platinum level. You meet every kind of personality in interviewers—from really sharp people to those who know nothing about the music. With ZZ, it really didn't matter. It was like switching on a light, instantly charming, friendly, relaxed. Everybody went away with a good story. Do you hold kind of informal coaching sessions?

LP: When I start to work with people we will go out and have dinner. We'll come to the office, start to hang out a little so I can get a feel for who they are. Then there are people who coach professionally, in how to do an interview. I generally hire one of those people to work, depending on the personality. In addition, I give them guidelines. I sit and talk to them. Sometimes if they are still a little uncomfortable, we can do a mock interview, so I can see their strengths and weaknesses. I can give them something on paper, which really helps. I might say, "Stop rambling, answer the question and stop talking." Or, "Don't say 'uh' all the time," or "If you are doing something for television you wiggle around too much."

Keep eye contact with the person interviewing, don't look at the camera. . . .
LP: Exactly.

Because the camera is going to move.
LP: If it's a group, when one member is talking, don't fidget and look away, because you might look bored.

That's deadly. You have to keep in mind, particularly for national television and radio, how important every second of footage and air time is—so you don't end up on the cutting room floor, replaced by some other act.
LP: Yes, CNN for example, they are coming to get something specific and it's only going to be a couple of minutes.

Let's talk about how you get your share of mainstream media. What are some ways you explore that? Say, you have an artist who is ready for "CNN Entertainment" or ready for Spin.
LP: I am the queen of followup. I think it is really important to send people every little thing that your artist is doing that could be interesting. From chart positions to visiting a women's shelter or visiting with kids, whatever. That can pull in the mainstream media, if they feel something is happening with your act. A lot is chart-based, that we all know. Even when an artist is high on the chart, you still have to trudge along and keep calling and keep giving more information.

I also find that working through freelancers is really good. If you can get a freelancer who is really into your project, they can work it through a lot of different outlets.

They will end up with a more exciting story because they are into it. The feel of the story will be better.
LP: Getting people music as early as possible and getting them to start thinking about it is the best route. Especially with rap or R&B acts, you have to build from the underground base and build up. I think it's important if an editor sees something about your group in say, *The Source*, they may think, "Okay, kids are into this, so maybe this is something that could be of mainstream interest."

Yes, even a small item can generate larger press. A word on professional relationships?
LP: A lot of my career has been based on breaking acts. To me it's really important to keep good relationships, going out to lunch, just calling people to say hello, even if you don't have anything special for them.

And doing favors that don't necessarily pertain to you or your office; for instance, a pair of tickets. People remember that.

LP: I was at lunch with an editor at *People*. He mentioned he loved Al Greene music. I found an Al Greene Christmas album and sent it to him.

That will come back to you, in a positive sense. You do have to be careful with requests. You can easily build up pester points if you overdo it.

LP: I see what a lot of publicists do wrong. Don't call somebody ten times. If you keep getting someone's machine and you keep leaving messages, they are going to get annoyed. You leave a couple of messages and then you call until you get them.

Honesty is important, too. You can say, this is not a great record, but I think it might be something that might happen. Don't tell people you "love" things. Every record that you have is not an earth-shattering release.

Publicist Howard Bloom was very professional about talking bad news. If I did not get an issue of down beat *he would say, "Well, we tried. Next?"*

LP: I think that is the best you can do. I have known publicists who hang up on people, who yell at writers and editors because they are not into their act.

You will not last long in this industry behaving like that. The past fifteen years have shown that PR people can be professional. I try in this book to articulate that. Are you doing much in the electronic world?

LP: We are currently developing a website for Loose Cannon. This is quite exciting and I'm taking classes.

MARK PUCCI
Owner, Mark Pucci Media, Atlanta, Georgia

Let's get a little background information. You attended Memphis State, right?

MP: Right, it is now called the University of Memphis.

You had your own rock and roll magazine.

MP: Right. I wasn't publisher. I started doing some freelance work for a couple of underground newspapers in Memphis. After I graduated, I became the music editor for a Memphis paper called the *River City Review*.

In addition to that, I freelanced for some national publications and wrote for *Rolling Stone, Phonograph Record* magazine, *Zoo World,* a number of other national publications.

And then you went to Capricorn Records in 1974.

MP: I stayed there until October 1979. I started out a tour publicist and then eventually became national publicity director. In 1979, I moved up to Atlanta and started my own company, Mark Pucci Associates. I was there from 1979 until September 1991. Then I rejoined Capricorn in Nashville as vice president of publicity. Then I became senior vice president/general manager in July 1995. In January 1996 I returned to Atlanta and formed my own publicity company, Mark Pucci Media. My e-mail address is mpmedia@aol.com.

A lot has changed in the industry since my book first came out in 1989. If you could perhaps reflect on some of the changes that you've seen in the previous years.
MP: The basic premise of what publicity is and how it operates has not changed. It's the tools you use that have changed so much. It has become so necessary to have computers and e-mail. Now we use faxes for press releases and satellite press conferences. The business has become so much more hardware-oriented. It's a better way, faster way and much more efficient way to get the word out to your press targets.

The publicist has many more tools available.
MP: Today, the way my office operates, the basic premise is still very much the same way it was—in terms of grassroots operation. By that I mean we operate on a premise of what is called "artist development." We stay with our bands from the very early stages and we work a great deal of tour press for them.

We are a small enough company still, where we can give all our acts the personalized attention that enables them to feel like they always have someone working for them. We work every tour date of every band, every time. So you don't just have a window of two or three months—if you are, say, a baby band—where you get only the benefits of the publicity department pushing your latest album to the media. We stay with it constantly until the next album comes out and then we pick up the next album. It is a consistent effort of artist development and artist visibility.

Looking back, one of the aspects that made our old office at Capricorn so effective was that we treated everybody the same way. We would call back a college reporter. I presume that you have stayed with that philosophy.
MP: Definitely. The way our office is situated, we work everything from the college newspapers, fanzines, regionals, to the multi-regional all the way to the national publications. In fact, the way alternative music has developed over the past ten years, it has emanated initially from this do-it-yourself ethic. Now there's less structured arrangements, less production values, much more stripped down.

With that came the growth of a number of different fanzines (privately published periodicals) and different publications. These really appreciated that whole idea of what these bands were about musically. Those publications became very credible, and so there is a definite network of publications out there that have maintained their viability over the years, survived and prospered. They really mean a lot to fans of that kind of music. I think the fans tend to believe something when it appears in that type of publication—more so than they would, say, in a major music magazine. Those have more of a national clout, but to these core fans, the big magazines, to a certain extent, are sold out because of commercialism and advertising considerations.

It is kind of a cyclical thing. There was a rash of fanzines in the 1970s. Certain of those were instrumental in breaking acts who became major artists.
MP: Exactly.

What about the international scope. Are you looking at getting exposures in foreign markets?
MP: Definitely. We see the value of international business, not only in Canada but also in Europe and Japan. That is an area we're really trying to concentrate on. I've had quite a lot of experience with American acts touring in various European countries and Japan.

Over the years a number of my international students have mentioned to me that American pop music is tremendously popular in Malaysia, for example, and in Spain and various countries in South America. I even got a letter from a graduate student in Bosnia who'd just finished reading my book. This is an exciting time in the industry. On a musical note, what do you see coming around the bend?
MP: Everything is so cyclical in this business. You had a reemergence of country music. I think that has peaked. I see a lot more homogenization happening with music. I think we are seeing a return to really good solid playing. In the early 1980s and into the mid-'80s, you had that growth of very techno-oriented music, drum machines, synthesizers, and "click" dance tracks.

Electro-pop.
MP: There has been a very healthy return to bands, real playing and real musicians. I see a continuing of that return and, of course, we will see a reaction to that and we may go through another phase. Look at growth in popularity of bands like Hootie and the Blowfish and the Dave Matthews Band and Collective Soul.

The other thing that is really happening is radio—it just keeps fragmenting and splitting off. It seems like there is a new radio format each month. This volatility is a reaction to the recent history of American radio. You saw radio becoming so polarized in the kind of music they were playing. Stations were excluding a lot of music—if it did not fit into that structured format, it had no place to get played. Finally you saw a reaction to that, the reemergence of a couple of a new formats like Triple-A (Adult Album Alternative). Triple-A became a very popular format. It was an outgrowth of what in the sixties and seventies was basically rock radio.

Until the "consultant" got in on it and ruined what we knew as rock radio.
MP: The people who used to listen to that kind of music were basically abandoned. A lot of people went to country music because a lot of those bands that were sort of country-oriented, had no place to be heard. The country audience embraced them and so you had acts like Travis Tritt and others emerging. They were very much in an idiom that is not straight country—with the energy levels.

Yes, with slide guitar solos, they sound as much like the Allman Brothers Band as they do Conway Twitty. Have you heard anything about any new playback technology, perhaps beyond the CD?
MP: Well, you have digital audiotape (DAT), which was the supposed next technology, but there was a great deal of hesitation among consumers. Many people were slow to switch from vinyl to CDs—and they're reluctant to move again. I think you'll see digital audiotape make more inroads.

In the consumer marketplace?
MP: Exactly. I think the future of all this involves computers and sound bytes. Audio and video "clips" via the Web are now very popular with fans. Direct delivery, into the PC, of entire albums is not that far away. This will have an impact on the retail industry as we know it.

Okay. Your message to the kids of the world?
MP: Stay in school.

MARILYN GILLEN
Billboard Magazine

At the time of this conversation, Gillen was Interactive Editor at *Billboard*, Los Angeles. Since then she has been promoted to News Editor, *Billboard*, New York.

Let's get a little background on you.
MG: This beat is about two years old now. Prior to that I was our pro/audio technology editor. It's a fun beat. I like to do that, getting into the studio.

Where did you go to school?
MG: Florida State. I'm a Southerner, from Tampa. I majored in English literature. I worked for the *Tampa Tribune* and the *St. Petersburg Times*, then *Billboard*.

How does one describe the Internet to somebody from Mars?
MG: That's a good question. The Internet is not an "it" necessarily, it is an online network. Most people get confused by that. It is a collection of individual computers around the world. It was originally formed with the Cold War in mind, as

a way to keep the U.S. Defense Department up and running, assuming a nuclear bomb was dropped and one node was wiped out. It is actually a lot older than most people realize. It started in the sixties.

The time when it came into public consciousness was probably in the early to mid-'90s. Most people who have been online consumer-wise started with what we called a commercial service, such as CompuServe, America Online, and Prodigy. The Internet was more kind of a "techy" area where your mainstream consumers never really went because it was so hard to navigate. Then came the evolution of something called the World Wide Web, which is a more visual element.

The graphic arena.
MG: Exactly, and it is a lot easier to navigate. That really spurred what you saw in terms of the consumer application. Basically, whenever anybody refers to the Internet in terms of a record label, having online sites, they are talking about the World Wide Web—that's a way of describing the way they are on the Internet. Anybody can get in who has a multimedia computer. All you need is a computer modem. Most consumers have a 14,400 bps modem, but a lot of the new applications are probably going to demand a 28,800 and higher. The new applications that you are going to see, in terms of delivering Muzak and using things like Realaudio, tools that make it easier to access music and graphics and video online—they're going to require a 28,800. People are upgrading as well.

They are buying more expensive speakers, smarter and heavier sound cards, faster video boards, more RAM.
MG: Once you start, it's addictive. I have a really good computer, but every week I read about something new.

It's worse than race cars, if that is imaginable. You know, you can never get enough horsepower.
MG: Exactly, and as soon as you have bought it, there is something better and cheaper immediately afterward.

I understand there are a lot more programs coming into the marketplace that make it easier to gain access and navigate, in terms of browsing.
MG: Absolutely. Netscape is one you are going to hear about a lot. That is a really easy browser to use. But then there are some other technologies.

Please elaborate.
MG: There are some technologies that are very specific to the music industry. They basically involve something called "streaming." Right now, if you go into a Website and you want to listen to a thirty-second sample of a song—it used to be you had to download it into your computer. Generally, downloading would be five times as long as the sample—up to five minutes. People didn't want to do that.

Now there are technologies out there like Realaudio and Zing Streamworks that allow sort of instantaneous feed of audio. All you do is click a button and instantly access the music. It is just "point and click."

Electra uses it in its Website. A lot of radio stations are using that technology as well. It is actually broadcast online so that you can have live feeds of audio online. Those are some of the key technologies that set up the breakthrough of audio on the Internet.

I recently spoke with Mark Pucci, a longtime buddy of mine. He and I used to work together at the old Capricorn Records. Mark had a fascinating prediction, that people would soon get their music via computer—bypassing the retail side.

MG: That is a really fun issue. Right now, you are seeing some actual partial-delivery online. It is a very sticky issue, obviously, for the labels. They do not want to offend their retail base.

You are also seeing retailers going online. Blockbuster Music, Tower Records, and Musicland are selling online. Then there are a bunch of dedicated record stores online exclusively. The chains recognize the future.

Clearly this technology opens up all kinds of vistas for the publicist.

MG: I think a lot of the Web activity at the labels started in their publicity and marketing departments—before it got so institutionalized. They were the first ones to recognize that it is basically a direct PR pipeline. You don't have to depend on an editor at a newspaper agreeing to run something about your artist. You just put up your own article and you don't have to go through a radio station to play a song. You actually put the song online yourself. Industry people are really excited about that.

The publicist of today or the near future will have to keep abreast of this rapidly changing situation, this "haunted house."

MG: Right now, you see a fair number of independent publicists. They seem to be targeting bulletin boards. These are chat areas focused on specific topics or artists. The indies are going in and posting little snippets about so-and-so's playing here this week, or something about "this artist is doing this" or "has this album coming out."

That is one of the good things about the Web in general. You have all these niche markets that you can target. If there is a whole forum devoted to country music, that is a great place to post something about a country artist. Although, there is sometimes some backlash, in terms of those not welcoming what they consider commercial activities. Absolutely, for all the applications being used, publicity and promotion are probably the most useful, actually getting a return.

It's obvious, the tie-in. Your column is a must-read. How about some other suggestions, books, other periodicals, so people might stay on top of this mercurial arena?

MG: Certainly, *Wired* is just hip, cool, trendy reading.

I had a book called The Student's Guide to the Internet, *which looks pretty well done. Any other movement, predictions that you might be thinking about?*
MG: Specifically for the music industry—it breaks down two ways: the online world and then packaged media. Online, I think we'll see used increasingly for publicity, for marketing, and on a certain basis for A&R. It is being used for business-to-business applications. Warner Brothers set up an online radio forum, where it is actually soliciting radio programmers. It is putting up tip sheets and song clips for them.

On the other side, you are seeing the music industry getting into multimedia, in terms of packaged media, which is CD-ROM and CD-Pluses. That area is also going to grow a little more slowly, but the industry is definitely moving into this.

Years ago, publicists wracked their heads trying to think of different ways to expose a given act. These days the current generation of publicists will be scratching their heads, trying to think of more creative ways to use this technology.
MG: Absolutely. Look at the enhanced CD or CD-Plus, the compilation out from Arista. It was a new album of alternate versions of a song. You go into the multimedia section and it has clips from all other albums. It has a merchandising section where you can call an 800 number to order any of those albums. They are selling T-shirts. The idea of using basically one album as a catalog is a fascinating way to promote not just the artist but the back catalog as well.

Another question I have for you is what sort of delivery technology do you see in the near future. What is the storage and playback system beyond the CD?
MG: We'll stick with the CD-based technology for the short-term future. The migration right now is what is called an enhanced CD, which is basically a regular album that you can play in a regular CD deck, but if you put it in your computer CD drive you will get video, text, lyrics. That seems to be pretty clearly the interim step.

Labels are kind of dabbling in CD-ROM, which are just bigger versions of CD-Pluses. Certainly, the next step is what is called digital video discs or high-density CDs.

Any other thoughts?
MG: Another thing cool for publicists—on the Internet there are a lot of good rumor mills and dirt folders. If you are looking for a job it is a good place to look, or for some good gossip it is a good place to look.

Your crystal ball and the new technologies?
MG: I don't honestly foresee in my crystal ball any huge changes coming. In terms of online development right now, it is growing exponentially and I think it

will continue. We will see more and more interesting applications. The industry has been leading the consumer marketplace and the consumers are just catching up. They have their computers at home and are really getting excited about it. I think we are going to see a lot more activity.

Your message to the kids of the world?
MG: Get e-mail and use it.

INDEX

BillboardBooks

**THANK YOU FOR BUYING
A BILLBOARD BOOK.
IF YOU ENJOYED THIS
TITLE, YOU MIGHT WANT
TO CHECK OUT OTHER
BOOKS IN OUR CATALOG.**

**THE BILLBOARD BOOK OF
AMERICAN SINGING GROUPS:
A History, 1940-1990** *by Jay Warner*
The definitive history of pop vocal groups, from the doo wop of
Dion and the Belmonts, to the Motown hits of the Supremes, to
the surf sound of the Beach Boys, to the country rock of Crosby,
Stills and Nash. More than 350 classic acts spanning five decades
are profiled here, with fascinating information about each group's
career, key members, and musical impact as well as extensive
discographies and rare photos. A one-of-a-kind reference for
vocal group fans and record collectors alike. 544 pages. 80 photos. Paperback. $21.95. 0-8230-8264-4.

**THE BILLBOARD BOOK OF NUMBER ONE ALBUMS:
The Inside Story Behind Pop Music's
Blockbuster Records** *by Craig Rosen*
A behind-the-scenes look at the people and stories involved in
the enormously popular records that achieved Number One album
status in the Billboard charts. Inside information on over 400
albums that have topped the chart since 1956, plus new interviews with hundreds of superstar record artists as well as a wealth
of trivia statistics and other facts. 448 pages. 425 photos.
Paperback. $21.95. 0-8230-7586-9.

BillboardBooks

THE BILLBOARD BOOK OF NUMBER ONE HITS,
Third Edition, Revised and Enlarged *by Fred Bronson*
The inside story behind the top of the charts. An indispensable listing of every single to appear in the top spot on the Billboard Hot 100 chart from 1955 through 1991, along with anecdotes, interviews, and chart data. 848 pages. 800 photos. Paperback. $21.95. 0-8230-8297-0.

THE BILLBOARD BOOK OF TOP 40 ALBUMS,
Third Edition, Revised and Enlarged
by Joel Whitburn
The complete guide to every Top 40 album from 1955 to 1994. Comprehensive information on the most successful rock, jazz, comedy, country, classical, Christmas, Broadway, and film sound-track albums ever to reach the top of the Billboard charts. Includes chart positions, number of weeks on the chart, and label and catalog number for every album listed. 416 pages. 150 photos. Paperback. $21.95. 0-8230-7631-8.

THE BILLBOARD BOOK OF
TOP 40 COUNTRY HITS:
Country Music's Hottest Records,
1944 to the Present *by Joel Whitburn*
From the classic recordings of Hank Williams and Bob Wills, to enduring artists Patsy Cline and Tammy Wynette, to today's young superstars Garth Brooks and Shania Twain, the rich history of country music is documented in this comprehensive compilation of Billboard's Country Singles charts. Provides exhaustive data on every record to score at least one Top 40 hit. 562 pages. 96 photos. Paperback. $21.95. 0-8230-8289-X.

THE BILLBOARD BOOK OF TOP 40 HITS,
Sixth Edition, Revised and Enlarged
by Joel Whitburn
A perennial favorite, listing every single to reach the Top 40 of Billboard's weekly Hot 100 charts since 1955. Includes new chart data and expanded biographical information and trivia on artists listed. 800 pages. 300 photos. Paperback. $21.95. 0-8230-7632-6.

BillboardBooks

THE BILLBOARD BOOK OF ONE-HIT WONDERS,
Second Edition, Revised and Expanded
by Wayne Jancik
A one-of-a-kind rock and roll reference guide that charts the flip side of the pop music story. Uncovers the fascinating circumstances surrounding the rise to fame—and occasional rapid return to obscurity—of performers who had only one hit in Billboard's Top 40 charts. Contains over 100 new entries and a wealth of data and entertaining information that just can't be found elsewhere. A must for pop music fans and record collectors. 512 pages. 235 photos. Paperback. $21.95. 0-8230-7622-9.

THE BILLBOARD GUIDE TO HOME RECORDING,
Second Edition, Revised and Updated *by Ray Baragary*
The complete do-it-yourself reference to recording techniques and equipment options. Provides a step-by-step approach to producing high-quality tapes, demos, and CDs in a home studio. Includes information on recorders, mixers, microphones, and signal processors; recording basic tracks and overdubbing; expanding the home studio with MIDI; the development of General MIDI standards; and the use of computers in sequencing. 272 pages. 97 illustrations. Paperback. $19.95. 0-8230-8300-4.

THE REAL DEAL:
How to Get Signed to a Record Label From A to Z
by Daylle Deanna Schwartz
A new music industry primer offering crucial information and advice that any musician playing popular music and desiring a record deal needs to have. Includes an explanation of the roles of an agent, attorney, A&R person, producer, and manager; what copyright and music publishing are; the importance of doing live performance; ways to build a following; how to use networking to reach the right people; and the pros and cons of releasing an independent recording. Also contains advice from top creative and business professionals and a resource section. 256 pages. Paperback. $16.95. 0-8230-7611-3.

BillboardBooks

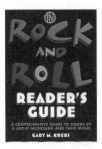

THE ROCK AND ROLL READER'S GUIDE
by Gary M. Krebs
An indispensable consumer guide for book collectors and music fans alike. The first comprehensive bibliography of books about, and by, rock and pop stars in addition to works written about the music scene itself. Focuses on both selected general reference works—such as artist profiles, chart data, pictorials, concert events, women and rock, and magazines—and all publications on artists A-Z. 464 pages. Paperback. $21.95. 0-8230-7602-4.

THIS BUSINESS OF ARTIST MANAGEMENT,
Revised and Enlarged Third Edition
by Xavier M. Frascogna, Jr. and H. Lee Hetherington
Firmly established as the standard reference work in the field of artist management in music, and winner of the 1980 Deems Taylor Book Award, this new edition of the title formerly known as Successful Artist Management offers the wise guidance and authoritative professional information required to develop an artist's career. Now revised and updated to include interviews with top record executives, coverage of new forms of business, updates on the legal framework of the music business, and contemporary investment and money management advice. 304 pages. Hardcover. $21.95. 0-8230-7705-5.

THIS BUSINESS OF MUSIC,
Seventh Edition by M. William Krasilovsky
and Sidney Shemel
The bible of the music business, with over 250,000 copies sold. A practical guide to the music industry for publishers, writers, record companies, producers, artists, and agents. Provides detailed information on virtually every economic, legal, and financial aspect of the complex business of music. 736 pages. Hardcover. $29.95. 0-8230-7755-1.

BILLBOARD'S HOTTEST HOT 100 HITS,
Revised and Enlarged Edition by Fred Bronson
The ultimate music trivia book. An illustrated compendium of 40 years of Billboard's chart data broken down into 175 categories, including artists, writers, producers, and record labels. Plus, a definitive list of the Top 5000 hits from 1955 through 1995. 512 pages. 250 photos. Paperback. $21.95. 0-8230-7646-6.

BillboardBooks

BLACK & WHITE BLUES:
Photographs by Marc Norberg,
edited by B. Martin Pedersen
From Graphis Publications, portraits of 60 of the finest blues
musicians of all time, accompanied by the artist's personal statement about the blues. A CD-ROM disc is packaged with the
hardcover edition. 192 pages. 60 photos. Hardcover (with CD):
$69.95. 0-8230-6471-9. Paperback: $45.95. 0-8230-6480-8.

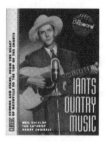

GIANTS OF COUNTRY MUSIC
Classic Sounds and Stars, from the Heart
of Nashville to the Top of the Charts
by Neil Haislop, Tad Lathrop, and Harry Sumrall
An inside view of country's biggest names, drawing upon dozens
of never-before-published interviews with such stars as Garth
Brooks, Mary Chapin Carpenter, and Willie Nelson. Each entry
focuses of the artist's career in detail and explains how their work
has fit into the surrounding musical landscape. 288 pages.
100 photos. Paperback. $21.95. 0-8230-7635-0.

GRAPHIS MUSIC CDS
edited by B. Martin Pedersen
This wide-ranging international collection from Graphis
Publications includes innovative covers, foldouts, inner sleeves,
and compact disk surfaces created by graphic designers special-
izing in cover and packaging design for music CDs. 224 Pages.
Over 300 illustrations. Hardcover. $75.95. 0-8230-6470-0.

KISS AND SELL:
The Making of A Supergroup *by C.K. Lendt*
A riveting expose of the machinations and manipulations of
what's involved in making it to the top of the rock world, written
by the man who traveled with Kiss for 12 years as their business
manager. Both a case study of the harsh realities of how the business of music works and a unique perspective on the lives,
lifestyles, and indulgences of rock stars. 352 pages. 18 photos.
Paperback. $18.95. 0-8230-7551-6.

BillboardBooks

MORE ABOUT THIS BUSINESS OF MUSIC,
Fifth Edition, Revised and Enlarged
by Sidney Shemel and M. William Krasilovsky
A completely updated companion to This Business of Music, this
book presents a practical guide to areas of the music business
such as jazz, religious music, live performances, the production
and sale of printed music, background music and transcriptions,
and the impact of technology from CDs and DATs to VCRs.
224 pages. Hardcover. $18.95. 0-8230-7642-3.

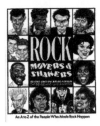

ROCK MOVERS AND SHAKERS:
An A-Z of the People Who Made Rock Happen, Revised
and Enlarged *by Dafyyd Rees and Luke Crampton*
An entertaining reference work identifying the most influential
and popular artists of the past 40 years. Documents the events of
artists' musical careers and personal lives chronologically. More
than 750 entries reveal what happened and when. 608 pages.
125 photos. Paperback. $19.95. 0-8230-7609-1.

The above titles should all be available from your neighborhood
bookseller. If you don't find a copy on the shelf, books can also
be ordered either through the store or directly from Watson-
Guptill Publications. To order copies by phone or to request
information on any of these titles, please call our toll-free number:
1-800-278-8477. To order copies by mail, send a check or money
order for the cost of the book, with $2.00 postage and handling
for one book and $ .50 for each additional book, plus applicable
sales tax in the states of CA, DC, IL, OH, MA, NJ, NY, PA, TN,
and VA, to:

WATSON-GUPTILL PUBLICATIONS
PO Box 2013
Lakewood, NJ 08701-9913